Up and Running!

A Comedy

Derek Benfield

A SAMUEL FRENCH ACTING EDITION

SAMUEL FRENCH

FOUNDED 1830

SAMUELFRENCH-LONDON.CO.UK
SAMUELFRENCH.COM

UP AND RUNNING!

First presented by Jack Watling Productions at the Frinton Summer Theatre, on 16th August, 1994, with the following cast:

Patrick Sumner	Paul Deitch
Trevor	Joseph Morton
Jenny	Rachel Scorgie
Reg Godfrey	Ian Soundy
Virginia	Ann Marcuson
Kate Sumner	Laura Jones

Directed by Susanna Harding

The action takes place in Patrick's flat in a fashionable part of London

ACT I	A Friday evening
ACT II	A few moments later

Time — the present

*Other plays by Derek Benfield
published by Samuel French Ltd:*

Anyone for Breakfast?
Bedside Manners
Beyond a Joke
A Bird in the Hand
Caught on the Hop!
Don't Lose the Place!
Fish Out of Water
Flying Feathers
In for the Kill
Look Who's Talking
Murder for the Asking
Off the Hook
Panic Stations
Post Horn Gallop
Running Riot
A Toe in the Water
Touch and Go
Wild Goose Chase

ACT I

Patrick Sumner's luxurious third-floor flat in a fashionable part of London. A Friday evening in the summer

The main door is R. There is a door leading into the kitchen, L, and in the far wall two other doors to the master bedroom and spare room. There is a large window overlooking the park, R, with a well-stocked drinks trolley in front of it. Further R there is a door leading to the bathroom. The furniture is comfortable and expensive and includes a sofa with a table behind it and a deep armchair. Various burgeoning house plants, equally burgeoning bookcases, and — rather incongruously — an exercise bicycle. The walls are adorned with modern paintings and various television awards

Pre-curtain music plays until the dialogue starts

Patrick is on his exercise bicycle, dressed in colourful shorts and a vest. He is a good-looking, well-preserved man of about fifty. He is a little tired, having been cycling for some time. The doorbell rings. Patrick ignores it, puffing heavily. It rings again

Patrick Go away! (*He continues cycling*)

The door is pushed open and Trevor comes in, carrying a very pretty girl in his arms. Trevor is an attractive young man, but at the moment he is looking a little distraught

Patrick is facing the other way and does not see them

Trevor I say, Patrick ——
Patrick I told you to go away! Can't you see I'm on a bicycle?
Trevor Good heavens, so you are!

Trevor sees that Patrick is on a bicycle

Patrick You mean you hadn't noticed?
Trevor Well, I do have other things on my mind ... !
Patrick You should know never to speak to a man on a bicycle. Especially when he's in the middle of Green Park.
Trevor Is *that* where you are?
Patrick I've done ten miles so far.

Trevor Oh, splendid! Well, I'm just going.

Patrick Good.

Trevor (*indicating the girl in his arms helplessly*) Is it all right if I leave this here for a minute?

Patrick (*busy bicycling*) Leave anything you like only get the hell out of here.

Trevor Right.

Trevor puts the young lady down on the sofa

(*To her*) I shan't be long.

Patrick There's no hurry. I'm not stopping till I get to Knightsbridge. (*He pedals, energetically*)

Trevor (*to her*) Now promise me you'll stay there.

Patrick Well, I'm not likely to go out in the street dressed like this, am I? (*He laughs*)

Trevor blows a kiss to the girl

Trevor Goodbye, darling!

Patrick Oh, Trevor! I didn't know you cared. (*He laughs*)

Trevor grins at the girl and goes out through the main door

Patrick is getting a bit short of breath but continues bicycling. The girl — Jenny — watches him for a moment with an amused smile

Jenny Have you got as far as Knightsbridge yet?

Patrick is startled by the sound of a female voice. Without turning around, he gradually slows down. Then he slowly turns to look where the voice came from. He sees Jenny and remains motionless, staring at her. She smiles nicely

Hallo ...

Patrick falls off his bicycle. He gets up and gazes at her in surprise

Patrick I thought you were a parcel.

Jenny No. I'm a person.

Patrick I can see that now!

Jenny I'm a girl.

Patrick I do know the difference. But when Trevor said he wanted to leave something I assumed it was a parcel.

Jenny No. It was me.

Patrick (*going to her*) Don't you mind being abandoned alone in a strange man's flat? *Anything* might happen to you.

Jenny (*hopefully*) Might it?

Patrick You don't know that I'm a nice, kind, honest, respectable, upright, good-natured, attractive, happily-married, married man. I might be a wild beast, seething with passion, ready to take advantage of you.

Jenny (*smiling, optimistically*) Oooh — are you really?

Patrick Of course I'm not!

Jenny What a pity. I expect you're too tired after cycling all the way to Knightsbridge. (*She giggles at his appearance*)

Patrick (*realizing he is in his shorts and vest*) Oh, my God! You're not supposed to see me like this!

Jenny Why not?

Patrick It's bad for my image. (*He goes quickly to grab his dressing-gown from the armchair and puts it on, trying to regain his dignity*)

Jenny (*with a smile*) Oh, yes. We mustn't forget your image, must we?

Patrick Well, I wasn't expecting a visitor! Not *yet*, anyway. (*He hastens across to pick up a towel from the exercise bicycle and dries his hot face and neck*)

Jenny Do you go in for that a lot?

Patrick Go in for what?

Jenny Riding a bicycle without moving.

Patrick I *was* moving!

Jenny The bicycle wasn't.

Patrick The bicycle doesn't *have* to move. The bicycle's quite happy where it is. *I'm* the one who wants the exercise. (*He continues mopping his brow*)

Jenny Seems silly riding a bicycle in the middle of the sitting-room. Why don't you get a real one and ride it outside?

Patrick Because I don't want people staring at me but I do need the exercise.

Jenny So I noticed.

She looks, pointedly, at his stomach. He pats it self-consciously

Patrick It's not as bad as all that!

Jenny Is that why you always wear loose-fitting jackets on the telly?

Patrick smiles, flattered

Patrick Ah! You've seen me on the television?

Jenny Every Saturday night.

Patrick preens himself

Patrick Oh, good! (*He sets off for the drinks trolley*)
Jenny My mother's a great fan of yours.
Patrick (*smarting*) Let me tell you, young lady, that over forty per cent of
the audiences for my chat shows are under thirty and over eighty per cent
are under fifty! (*He pours some orange juice*)
Jenny Well, that's more than *you* are.
Patrick I'm nowhere *near* fifty! (*He drinks some juice, defiantly*)
Jenny You're nowhere near thirty, either ... In fact, some of the newspapers
have been saying that you're past it.

Patrick turns

Patrick (*bridling*) Past it? I'm in my prime! Just because I ride a stationary
bicycle in my sitting-room does not mean that I'm a geriatric!
Jenny Well, you fell off it when you saw *me*.
Patrick That had nothing to do with my age! You gave me a shock. I was
expecting to see a parcel, so I was rather surprised to see a strange girl
instead.
Jenny I'm Jenny. How do you do. (*She holds out her hand*)
Patrick How do you do. (*He shakes her hand, automatically*)
Jenny There! Now I'm not a strange girl anymore, am I? (*She smiles,
delightedly*)
Patrick (*retaining immunity*) I still want to know what the hell you're doing
in my flat. (*He finishes off his drink*)
Jenny Waiting for Trevor.
Patrick Well, you can't wait here! I've got someone coming for drinks and
I want to get dressed. So you must go! (*He thumps down his empty glass
on the drinks trolley*)
Jenny I can't. I've twisted my ankle.
Patrick Oh, my God ... !
Jenny That's why Trevor carried me into your flat.
Patrick (*returning a little*) Why didn't he carry you into his *own* flat?
Jenny He refused.
Patrick Doesn't sound like Trevor. He wouldn't refuse a woman unless she
was ugly or eighty. And you're neither.
Jenny (*pleased*) Ah — you noticed?
Patrick Well ... yes — of course I noticed.
Jenny Oh, good! (*She smiles at him, delightfully*)
Patrick (*avoiding her eyes in his towel*) So how did you twist your ankle,
then?

Jenny I ... I tripped on the stairs. I think I've sprained it ... (*She suffers, suitably*)

Patrick And Trevor left you sitting on the stairs with a sprained ankle?

Jenny Yes.

Patrick Good God ... !

Jenny (*the wronged woman*) I think he had another girl in there ...

Patrick (*quietly*) I wouldn't be surprised ... ! Look — I'm very sorry about your ankle ...

Jenny (*cheering up immediately*) Oh, thank you, Patrick.

Patrick But I've got to get dressed, so you really must go!

Jenny But I can't walk ... Trevor carried me in, so he'll have to carry me out. (*Then with a hopeful smile*) Unless *you'd* like to carry me?

Patrick (*advancing, impatiently*) Oh, all right.

He encounters her welcoming arms and retreats instantly

No, *not* all right!

Jenny I suppose you're too tired after all that pedalling?

Patrick It's nothing to do with pedalling!

Jenny Oh — you're frightened of touching me, is that it?

Patrick Of course I'm not frightened of touching you! (*But he is*) But I can't go out there dressed like this. (*He puts his towel down on the exercise bicycle*)

Jenny I know you *talk* a lot about sex on your telly show, but perhaps it's different when you come face-to-face with it.

Patrick I do *not* talk about sex on my show! (*He moves his exercise bicycle away a little*)

Jenny Yes, you do. The other night you had a scientist on the programme and you got so excited I thought you were going to fall off your chair, and he was only talking about the mating habits of frogs.

Patrick (*simmering*) I was being polite and paying attention.

Jenny You were opening your eyes so wide you were beginning to *look* like a frog.

Patrick For somebody who doesn't like my programme you seem to watch it an awful lot. (*He paces away round the sofa*)

Jenny Who said I didn't like it? I watch it every week.

Patrick (*bitterly*) With your mother!

Jenny No. I watch it on my own.

Patrick (*pleased*) Do you really? Oh, good! (*He smiles, enjoying the flattery, and perches on the back of the sofa, facing her*)

Jenny And *I* don't think your career's fading at all.

Patrick (*brittle*) Who said it was?

Jenny There was an article in the paper the other day. It said you were on your way out.

Patrick You shouldn't believe what you read in the newspapers.

Jenny gazes at him, thoughtfully

Jenny Y'know, Patrick — you're not a bit like you are on the telly. You're quite different in the flesh.

Patrick You weren't supposed to see me in the flesh! (*He gets up and stalks away from her*)

Jenny (*without malice*) In fact ... you're quite ordinary really, aren't you?

Patrick hesitates, uncertainly

Patrick Is that meant to be a compliment?

Jenny I suppose *you* think you're far from ordinary?

Patrick (*modestly*) Well, I ... I did think I had a bit more than most men.

Jenny (*giggling*) No wonder you were doing exercises!

Patrick (*smarting*) I do exercises to *keep* my figure, not to regain it.

Jenny Well, if *you* aren't going to carry me I'll just have to settle down here until Trevor comes to collect me. (*She settles herself amongst the cushions*)

Patrick (*going to her in alarm*) No! No — you can't do that!

Jenny Why are you so nervous? Are you frightened that your wife's going to come home and find me here?

Patrick She's not likely to do that.

Jenny Why not?

Patrick Because she's about thirty thousand feet up there. (*He points heavenwards*)

Jenny (*sadly*) Oh, dear. I'm sorry. I didn't realize ...

Patrick Realize what?

Jenny That your wife's dead ...

Patrick (*laughing*) Of course she's not dead!

Jenny Isn't that what you meant?

Patrick Good Lord, no! I think heaven is a bit more than thirty thousand feet up. She's flying to Paris.

Jenny Without *you*?

Patrick She's a dress designer. She goes there on business.

Jenny smiles, delighted

Jenny So you're here on your own?

Patrick Yes, but ——

Jenny Good! I'll keep you company.

Patrick No, you won't! (*He moves away from her*)

Jenny Why not? Don't you fancy me?

Patrick I'm expecting someone for drinks!

Jenny I see. The minute your wife's out of the way you invite a girlfriend in!

Patrick I haven't *got* a girlfriend! The person I'm expecting is the new boss of the television company I work for, so I want to make a good impression on him.

Jenny Why? Does *he* think your career's fading?

Patrick Of course he doesn't! (*Then he loses heart*) Well ... I *hope* he doesn't ... ! But he's a very puritanical man, so I don't want him marching in here and finding a pretty girl like you stretched out on my sofa!

Jenny You do think I'm pretty, then?

Patrick Of course I think you're —— That's got nothing to do with it! He might jump to conclusions. So by the time I've had a cold shower and put my clothes back on I want *you* to have disappeared! (*He plonks the telephone into her lap, abruptly*) There you are. Call Trevor. Double three-five-four. Tell him to come up here at once and collect his girl-in-waiting!

Patrick stalks majestically out into the bathroom

Jenny grins happily, puts the telephone aside, gets up and runs without difficulty to the exercise bicycle. Smiling mischievously, she gets on to it and experiments with a little pedalling. The doorbell rings. Jenny leaps off the exercise bicycle and races back to resume her position on the sofa. The doorbell rings again

Patrick's head pops out of the bathroom

That'll be Trevor! Tell him to come in and to stop ringing the bloody doorbell!

His head disappears back into the bathroom

Jenny (*calling*) Come in and stop ringing the bloody doorbell!

The door opens carefully and Reg Godfrey comes in. He is a severe man in his fifties, heavy with the responsibility of position and power. He carries a briefcase

He sees Jenny on the sofa. And she sees him. Which is not what either of them expected

Jenny Oh!

Reg Ah ... (*Pause*) You did say to come in?

Jenny Yes.

Reg And to stop ringing the —— ?

Jenny Yes. But I wasn't expecting *you* ...

Reg (*staring at her in surprise*) And *I* wasn't expecting *you*! I think I must be in the wrong flat. (*He goes back towards the door*)

Jenny What number did you want?

Reg Twenty-eight.

Jenny Then you *aren't* in the wrong flat.

Dark suspicion descends upon Reg Godfrey, and suits him very well. He closes the door and comes back into the room a little, looking at the very pretty girl on the sofa

You selling insurance or something?

Reg No, no, no, I'm ——

Jenny (*apprehensively*) You're not the press, are you?

Reg No, I'm not the press either. I'm ——

Jenny That's all right, then. Patrick's not very fond of the press at the moment. They've been saying the most dreadful things about him!

Reg (*grimly*) Yes, I know. I read them! (*He moves nearer to her*) So this is what happens!

Jenny What?

Reg When the cat's away ...

Jenny Sorry?

Reg Out of sight, out of mind.

Jenny racks her brains and tries to join in

Jenny It's a long road that has no turning?

Reg I didn't expect the famous Patrick Sumner to go in for *this* sort of thing ...

Jenny What sort of thing?

Reg That's how it looks!

Jenny Oh, no. It's not as good as it looks.

Reg What?!

Jenny (*hastily correcting herself*) As *bad* as it looks!

Reg Then why are you lying down on the sofa in his flat?

Jenny Because I'd sprained my ankle. Look — it's all swollen! (*She holds up her foot for inspection*)

Reg (*holding up his briefcase to prevent his eyes from settling on her leg*)
No! Take it away! I don't want to see it! (*Grimly*) I think I'd better have a
word with Mr Sumner ...

Jenny Well, you can't.

Reg Why not?

Jenny Because he's out there having a cold shower and putting his clothes
back on.

Reg I can't think why he took his clothes off in the first place!

Jenny Well, he was ever so hot, you see — after his exertions. If you ask me,
I think he's too old for it.

Reg I beg your pardon?!

Jenny For riding on his bicycle. (*She indicates the exercise bicycle*)

Reg turns and sees it

Reg Oh. Oh, I see ... (*He studies the exercise bicycle perfunctorily*)

Jenny (*reaching for a writing pad and pen*) Would you care to leave a
message?

Reg No, I would not!

Jenny (*pen poised*) Who shall I say called?

Reg I'm Reg Godfrey! And Mr Sumner's expecting me!

Jenny You're not his new boss, are you?

Reg Yes, I am!

*Jenny puts down the pad and pen and glares at Reg in unabashed remonstra-
tion*

Jenny Well, you're early. He wasn't expecting you so soon.

Reg No — I can see that! I didn't expect to arrive here and find young ladies
with legs lying about on sofas!

Jenny (*defiantly*) Only *one*!

Reg (*appalled*) One leg?

Jenny One lady!

Reg That's quite enough to be going on with! (*Prowling, grimly*) So this is
what he gets up to when his wife's away in Paris ... (*He puts his briefcase
down in the armchair*)

Jenny Here — you don't think —— ?

Reg Yes, I *do* think! Sumner's show has always been squeaky clean, so the
last thing *he* can afford is scandal!

Jenny Well, we mustn't have any of *that*, then, must we, Reg? (*Casually*)
You ... you haven't *met* his wife, I suppose?

Reg is puzzled by this apparent volte-face

Reg No. Not yet.
Jenny (*smiling happily*) That's what I thought!
Reg Poor woman ...
Jenny Thank you, Reg.
Reg Not you! Her!
Jenny Oh, you are silly ... !
Reg Sorry?
Jenny Didn't you realize? (*She holds out her hand, graciously*) Jenny
    Sumner. How do you do.

Reg stares at her in surprise

Reg You ... you mean ... ? (*He is about to take her hand, then thinks the better
    of it and retreats*) No — you couldn't be!
Jenny Why not?
Reg Well, you've ... (*he waves a hand vaguely towards her legs*) ... you've
    got ...
Jenny These? Oh, these are legs.
Reg Yes — I know!
Jenny Don't wives *have* legs?
Reg Not like those ... ! (*He escapes around the sofa*)
Jenny (*getting into her stride*) Patrick spotted me when I was in the chorus.
Reg I'm not surprised!
Jenny He sent flowers to me at the stage door. (*Romantically*) Two dozen
    red roses ... every day for two weeks. Well, after that I just *had* to marry him,
    didn't I?
Reg You ... you really *are* his wife?
Jenny Yes, of course.
Reg How awful!
Jenny What?
Reg Not you! *Me*! You see, I thought ——
Jenny Yes — I know what you thought! Oh, Reg, you are naughty!
Reg And that's why you didn't go to Paris? Because you'd twisted your ...
    (*He indicates her ankle*)
Jenny Ankle. Yes — exactly!

Reg sits beside her

Reg (*confidentially*) May I be frank with you, Mrs Sumner?
Jenny You must call me Jenny ...

Reg Well, Jenny ... you're not quite what I expected.

Jenny Aren't I?

Reg You're much younger than I thought you'd be. Nobody told me that the famous TV star Patrick Sumner had been cradle-snatching! (*He laughs, sycophantically*)

Jenny You mustn't let *him* hear you say that ...

Reg Well, after all, how old is old Patrick? Must be fifty if he's a day.

Jenny He'd never admit it!

Reg Nothing wrong with being fifty. I've been fifty myself before now.

Jenny (*flattering him*) Oh, *surely* not? Forty-five possibly. But never fifty.

Reg smiles, enjoying her attention

Reg You know, I think I'm going to like you.

The telephone near Jenny rings. She looks at it, uncertainly. A pause. It continues to ring. She does not move. Reg smiles

Aren't you going to answer it?

Jenny (*nervously*) Do you think I should?

Reg (*laughing*) Why not? It is your flat. You do live here! Ha! Ha! Ha!

Jenny Ah — yes — of course! I quite forgot! (*She picks up the telephone and assumes a deep voice*) Patrick Sumner's residence. (*In her normal voice*) Oh, it's you ... You want me to what? Well, I can't! I've sprained my ankle. (*She smiles at Reg, then reacts in alarm at what the caller — Trevor — is saying*) No! No — you mustn't do that! It's not convenient! ... No — no, listen —— ! (*But Trevor has hung up, so she puts down the telephone and looks at Reg, sheepishly*) The window-cleaner. He's coming up to collect his money!

Reg (*puzzled by her vehemence*) Nothing wrong with that, is there? Poor man's got to be paid.

Jenny I think I'll go into the bedroom! (*She gets up, abruptly, forgetting about her ankle*)

Reg (*alarmed for her*) Ankle!!

Jenny Aaaah!

She throws herself back on to the sofa in spectacular agony, ending up in his arms

I'd forgotten! Meeting you put it out of my head. (*Gazing into his eyes*) Will you carry me, then?

Reg Sorry?

Jenny Into the bedroom.
Reg Well ... I ...
Jenny Don't you think you can do it?
Reg What?
Jenny I'm not very heavy.
Reg No, I'm sure you're not, but ——
Jenny Pick me up, then!

Reg disentangles himself from her and makes his escape, tidying his clothes

Reg Patrick'll be here in a minute.
Jenny And so will the other one ... ! (*She looks anxiously towards the door*)
Reg It's only the window-cleaner.
Jenny Yes, but I don't want him to see me!
Reg (*puzzled*) Why not?
Jenny He's always looking at my legs! So, come on, Reg — carry me into
   the bedroom!
Reg (*with a resigned smile*) Oh, very well. I can see you're not a woman to
   be trifled with. (*He goes to her*) But promise me you'll join us later for a
   drink.
Jenny Yes, of course! Once Trevor's out of the way ...
Reg Trevor?
Jenny Er — the window-cleaner! Come on! Don't hang about! (*She holds
   out her arms, encouragingly*)
Reg Oh. Yes. Right.

Still somewhat embarrassed, Reg lifts her up in his arms

Now, then — which way to the bedroom?

Jenny hesitates

Jenny Er ... I think it's through there.
Reg You don't sound very certain! Ha! Ha! Ha!
Jenny Well, we dress designers spend so much time travelling from place
   to place one does tend to forget which bedroom one is in.
Reg Yes, I bet you do! Ha! Ha! Ha! I say — you're as light as a feather.
Jenny That's because *you're* so strong ...

Reg preens himself sheepishly, and sets off towards the bedroom

Reg Let's try through here, then, shall we?

Jenny Right, Reg!

Reg Sumner's a lucky man, you know. Where did he manage to find *you*?

Jenny (*blithely*) Oh, he just turned around and there I was ...

Reg carries her out into the bedroom, laughing

The moment they have gone, Trevor races in, looking for Jenny

Trevor Look, will you stop messing about! You can't stay up here, and I'm rather —— (*He stops in front of the sofa, seeing nobody there*) Good heavens ... !

Puzzled, he picks up Jenny's handbag, wondering where its owner can be. He looks about, still holding the handbag

Where the hell has she got to ... ?

Reg returns and sees Trevor the window-cleaner

Reg Ah!

Trevor jumps a mile as he sees a stranger coming out of Patrick's bedroom

Trevor Aaaah!

Reg crosses, busily, to Trevor

Reg So *you're* the one who's always looking at her legs! How much does she owe you? (*He reaches into his pocket*)

Trevor I beg your pardon?

Reg You are the window-cleaner, I presume? Come to collect your money.

Trevor Do I *look* like a window-cleaner?

Reg notices that Trevor is carrying a lady's handbag

Reg I don't know *what* you look like!

Trevor (*posturing, proudly*) I'm a friend of Patrick's!

Reg So am I.

Trevor I live downstairs. The flat under this one.

Reg (*apprehensively*) You're not joining us for dinner, are you?

Trevor Well, that's very kind of you but I'm a bit busy downstairs at the moment.

Reg Then what are you doing up here?

Trevor I left something behind.

Reg Well, you seem to have found it! (*He points to the handbag*)

Trevor What? (*He remembers he is still carrying the handbag*) No — not this! I didn't leave *this* behind! (*He tries, unsuccessfully, to hide the handbag behind his back*)

Reg *Always* carry it, do you?

Trevor Of course not!

Reg Not your colour, perhaps?

Trevor It doesn't belong to *me*! It belongs to a friend of mine.

Reg Just lent it to you for the evening, has he?

Trevor It's not a *he*, it's a *she*!

Reg And what did you lend her in return? Bowler hat and a rolled umbrella? Well, don't stay here on my account! If you're busy downstairs you'd better pick up whatever you came to collect and be on your way.

Trevor But that's the trouble. I don't know where it is! (*He looks about for the missing Jenny*)

Reg Well, where did you leave it?

Trevor Over there, but it's gone! (*Going to him*) You ... you didn't notice anything ... lying about, did you?

Reg What sort of thing?

Trevor (*smiling, dreamily*) Oh ... soft and sweet and pink ...

Reg (*enthusiastically*) Box of marshmallows?

Trevor Better than that!

Reg Better than marshmallows?

Trevor Oh, yes.

Reg I can't think of anything better than marshmallows ... (*He thinks about marshmallows*)

Trevor A girl.

Reg A *girl*?!

Trevor You didn't see a spare one hanging about, did you?

Reg begins to inflate. He glares at Trevor

Reg No, I did not! You won't find spare girls hanging about in Patrick Sumner's flat!

Trevor But I left her up here!

Reg Up *here*?! Whatever for?

Trevor Because I didn't want her downstairs in *my* flat. (*He goes towards the spare room, looking about*)

Reg, a stranger to such immorality, is appalled

Reg Why are you looking for a girl if you don't want her?

Trevor I do want her. But not now. I've got another one down there already.

Reg (*reeling*) Another girl?

Trevor Well, I wasn't expecting this one, you see. She just turned up on my doorstep. So I had to leave her up here for the time being while I got myself sorted out downstairs. You know how it is.

Reg escapes quickly from the source of such sinful thoughts

Reg No, I do *not* know how it is! Are you trying to tell me that you've got a surplus of girlfriends?

Trevor (*following him, modestly*) Well ... yes. Occasionally I do get a double booking. So if there's an overflow I leave one of them up here with Patrick.

Reg And what does Patrick do with her?

Trevor Keeps her entertained, I suppose.

Reg (*clutching the exercise bicycle for support*) Entertained?! How?

Trevor Gives a drink. Some nuts or something. *I* don't know, do I?

Reg I hope the press doesn't get to hear about this!

Trevor What have the press got to do with it?

Reg You know what the tabloids are like. Always infiltrating the homes of the famous — hoping for a headline. If they've seen you bringing girls in and out of Patrick's flat you can imagine what *they'll* make out of it! They've already started criticizing his programme, so the last thing he can afford at the moment is a scandal.

Trevor But there *isn't* any scandal.

Reg There is if the press *says* there is! (*Going to him*) Doesn't Sumner mind being left alone up here with your surplus?

Trevor Oh, no. I think he enjoys it.

Reg Enjoys it?!

Trevor Provided his wife doesn't find out.

Reg But she will.

Trevor She won't!

Reg She might!

Trevor She mustn't!

Reg Poor little thing ...

Trevor Oh, thank you.

Reg Not you — *her*!

Trevor Who?

Reg Patrick's wife! I can't bear to think how *she'll* feel when she finds out about your little ... "arrangement".

Trevor Don't be daft! We're not going to tell her.

Reg She'll find out!

Trevor She won't!
Reg She might!
Trevor She mustn't!
Reg (*grimly*) I expected Patrick Sumner to be a man above reproach ... (*He collects his briefcase and starts to leave*)
Trevor Where are you going? I thought you were here to have a drink with Patrick.
Reg I need time to think ... before I drink ... with Patrick. Time to make a decision. (*He opens the door*)
Trevor Can I give him a message?
Reg Yes — tell him I've gone to the pub on the corner!

Reg goes, closing the door behind him

Trevor (*looking about*) She must be here *somewhere* ...

He goes into the kitchen

Patrick comes in from the bathroom. He is now dressed

Trevor returns from the kitchen

Patrick (*jumping in alarm at the sight of Trevor*) Aah! (*Recovering*) What are *you* doing up here? I thought you'd be busy downstairs by now.

During the following Patrick busily prepares for his drinks session with Reg

Trevor I shall be in a minute. But I've got a message for you first.
Patrick And *I've* got a message for *you*! From now on you've got to stop leaving girls lying about in my flat. (*He goes to the drinks trolley*)
Trevor Are you going to listen to this message or not?
Patrick I've got an important meeting tonight and the last thing I want is some of your spare sitting on my sofa!
Trevor What else was I supposed to do with her? (*Looking about*) Where the hell is she? (*He disappears behind the sofa, searching*)
Patrick (*turning*) You had no right to —— (*he finds that Trevor has disappeared*) *Now* where have you gone?

Trevor reappears from behind the sofa on his hands and knees

Ah! You had no right to do that to a man in my position.
Trevor Why? What position were you in?

Patrick In my shorts on a bicycle! (*He moves the drinks trolley further into the room*)

Trevor I expect she's seen men in shorts before. (*He gets to his feet and looks about*)

Patrick Not *me* she hasn't! Before she'd only seen me on the television.

Trevor Ah — now — before I forget ——

Patrick looks concerned, his mind elsewhere

Patrick Do *you* think I wear loose-fitting jackets?

Trevor What?

Patrick On my programme!

Trevor Can't say I've noticed. (*Going to him*) Now, listen — the thing is ——

Patrick (*suddenly suspicious*) You do watch my programme, don't you?

Trevor Yes, of course! Sometimes ...

Patrick What do you mean "sometimes"?

Trevor Off and on.

Patrick Off and on?!

Trevor Look — do you want this message or not?

Patrick stares at Trevor, deeply offended

Patrick You're supposed to be a friend of mine! And yet you only watch my programme "off and on"?

Trevor Well ... more on than off. As a matter of fact I quite often watch it. When I'm with a girlfriend.

Patrick What does that mean ... ?

Trevor Well ... sometimes we're on the sofa together ... and I watch your programme.

Patrick considers this with growing apprehension

Patrick You mean to say that when I'm giving my all on the television you're giving your all on the sofa?

Trevor (*defensively*) Well, at least I'm watching you! That's something, isn't it? (*He helps himself to nuts from the drinks trolley*)

Patrick You might at least concentrate! (*He slaps Trevor's wrist and removes the dish of nuts from him*)

Trevor Why? It doesn't make any difference to your ratings, does it? The television company doesn't ring me after your show and ask if I was concentrating or not. (*He moves towards the bathroom*)

Patrick Well, what about *your* ratings? Doesn't your female companion suggest that you stop watching me and concentrate on *her*?

Trevor Oh, no. *She's* watching you as well.

Patrick reels, appalled at the thought

Patrick I wonder if this is happening all over the country ... ? I'll never be able to look the camera in the lens again. I shall feel like a Peeping Tom!

He staggers out into the kitchen

Trevor, who has more important things on his mind, looks hopefully into the bathroom

Trevor You in there? (*He can find no trace of her and closes the door. Calling to Patrick*) What the hell did you do with her?
Patrick (*off*) Who?
Trevor The girl I left on your sofa!

Patrick returns from the kitchen with a tray of ice cubes and an ice bucket

Patrick I didn't do anything with her! I put on my dressing-gown and went and had a cold shower.
Trevor Why? Were you over-excited?
Patrick (*glaring at Trevor*) I had a shower because I had just been cycling from Charing Cross to Knightsbridge. (*He goes to the drinks trolley and puts the ice cubes into the ice bucket*)
Trevor But where did you put her?
Patrick Jenny?
Trevor Is that her name?
Patrick (*appalled*) You don't even know her name?
Trevor Well, I only met her the other day in the supermarket. We got into conversation over the frozen fish. You know how it is.
Patrick No, I do not! I'm not in the habit of socializing in Sainsbury's. Anyway, why did you dump her on *my* sofa?
Trevor Because I'd got another one downstairs on *my* sofa. (*He grabs some more nuts and escapes towards the sofa*)
Patrick Another girl?!
Trevor Yes. She comes from Finsbury Park.
Patrick And I don't suppose you know *her* name, either!
Trevor Yes, I do! It's Virginia.
Patrick So why did you invite Jenny tonight when you'd already got another one arriving from Finsbury Park?
Trevor I didn't know Jenny was coming tonight!
Patrick I thought you'd fixed a date amongst the frozen fish?

Trevor Oh, we hadn't made a definite arrangement. She just turned up out of the blue.

Patrick So now Virginia's on her way back to Finsbury Park?

Trevor No. She's downstairs in my flat.

Patrick You mean she's still there!

Trevor Oh, yes. First come, first served.

Patrick So now you've got two of them?

Trevor No, no. Just one. Virginia.

Patrick So what have you done with Jenny?

Trevor Nothing. I've got to get rid of her.

Patrick (*going to him*) But Jenny isn't here anymore!

Trevor Isn't she?

Patrick You came back and fetched her!

Trevor No, I didn't.

Patrick I heard the doorbell.

Trevor No, no! When I came in just now your friend was here on his own.

Patrick I haven't got a friend here.

Trevor Of course you have! That's what I've been trying to tell you.

Patrick What are you talking about?

Trevor He said you were expecting him for drinks.

Patrick (*horrified*) Oh, my God! Don't say he arrived early and found Jenny on my sofa!

He grabs Trevor and clutches him, frantically

What did he look like?

Trevor Well, he was sort of ... (*he mimes a tall person*)

Patrick Tall?

Trevor Yes. With a ... (*he mimes a moustache*)

Patrick Moustache?

Trevor Yes. And — er ... (*he mimes spectacles*)

Patrick Glasses?

Trevor Yes.

Patrick dramatically casts Trevor aside on to the sofa

Patrick Oh, my God — it's him!

Trevor God?

Patrick No, but you're getting warm! Reg Godfrey — my new boss! He's only just taken over as Controller of Programmes — and you know what he was before that? Head of Religious Broadcasting in Scotland!

Trevor Why have they put a man like that in charge?

Patrick Because Head Office have decided that it's time we had less sex and violence on television, and they think that Reg is just the man to bring back the old-fashioned standards of decency.

Trevor So what are *you* worried about? There's no sex and violence on your show. It's all *very* old-fashioned. (*He laughs*)

Patrick Trevor — I need to make a good impression. The slightest breath of scandal about me and I'll be out! For good! My career kaput!

Trevor You were only having a cold shower.

Patrick Yes. *You* know that, and *I* know that, but *he* doesn't know that, does he? Put yourself in his position! If you arrived here knowing my wife was in Paris and found a pretty girl with legs lying on my sofa what would *you* think?

Trevor I'd think you were after a bit of nookie.

Patrick You see what I mean! (*He paces away, wildly*)

Trevor But he *didn't* see her, did he?

Patrick (*alert, like a bird*) Didn't he? How do you know?

Trevor Because I asked him if he'd seen a spare girl hanging about in here and he said no.

Patrick (*returning to Trevor, his hopes rising*) You mean Jenny must have gone *before* Reg arrived?

Trevor Yes! She must have hopped out to the lifts and been going down as I was coming up.

Patrick Oh, splendid! That *is* good news! Trevor, you're a pal!

He kisses him on the forehead and returns happily to the drinks trolley, content in the knowledge that Jenny is out of the way. Trevor hastens to depart

Trevor (*hesitating briefly*) Anyway, even if he *had* seen her it wouldn't have mattered.

Patrick (*busy with his bottles*) Wouldn't it?

Trevor No. Because I told him that sometimes I off-loaded my spare birds on to you if there was a bottleneck downstairs.

Patrick You told him that?!

Trevor (*innocently*) Why not?

He opens the door and goes

Patrick runs out, pulls Trevor back inside and shuts the door

Patrick Trevor ... Trevor ... er ... Reg did realize that on these occasions I was just ... (*with a gesture*) ... helping you out, and not ... (*another gesture*) helping myself?

Trevor Oh, yes! (*Then, less certainly*) Well, I *think* so. I told him you didn't mind. As long as your wife didn't find out.

Patrick (*in horror*) You told him *what*?!

Trevor It's the truth, isn't it?

Patrick Not in the way you make it sound! Anyway, where's Reg *now*?

Trevor Ah, yes! He's gone to the pub on the corner to think things over and make a decision.

Patrick (*exploding*) Why the hell didn't you tell me that before?!

Trevor I *tried* to!

He opens the door to go, but Patrick pulls him back inside and shuts the door again

Patrick That's it! That's the end of my career!

Trevor Why?

Patrick (*pacing, wildly*) Because I know what moral men are like. Always prying into other people's morals! First thing on Monday morning he'll be up there on the sixth floor dictating my demise!

Trevor (*puzzled*) Sixth floor?

Patrick The executive floor of Television House! The place where they can finish a man's career before they've even had their morning coffee!

Trevor But why should Reg want to finish *your* career? Surely he's not going to take any notice of what half a dozen silly critics have been saying?

Once more Trevor opens the door hopefully, but Patrick slams it shut again

Patrick (*appalled*) Half a dozen? You mean there were six of them?! I only saw three. (*Doomed, he paces away again*) Oh, my God! If Reg has got any doubts about my show after reading those newspapers then the slightest suspicion of scandal will finish me off!

Trevor opens the door and tries to escape unnoticed. But Patrick has eyes in the back of his head

Where are you going?

Trevor Back to Virginia, of course.

Patrick But what about *me*?!

Trevor (*without enthusiasm*) Well, you can come if you like, but you'll only be in the way.

Patrick What am I going to do about *Jenny*!

Trevor But Jenny's gone! So you've got nothing to worry about.

He grins and goes quickly, closing the door behind him

Patrick, the fears of failure heavy on his shoulders, hastens to the drinks trolley and pours himself a whisky

As he pours, the bedroom door opens and Jenny looks in. She sees him and smiles

Jenny Can I come in now?

Patrick sees her and freezes in disbelief but continues pouring the whisky. Eventually, the whisky overflows and brings him round. He notices that he now has a full glass of whisky. He mops up the overflow with a cloth

Patrick I thought you'd gone!
Jenny How could I go when I've twisted my ankle?
Patrick You could have hopped! What the hell were you doing in there?
Jenny Hiding. I didn't want Trevor to know I was still here. But now he's gone, so that's all right, isn't it? (*She hops to the sofa and sits down, happily*)
Patrick No, it is *not* all right! (*He leaves his whisky and goes to her in panic*) You — you didn't *see* anyone, did you?
Jenny I told you — I was hiding from him.
Patrick Not Trevor! You didn't see anyone *else*?
Jenny (*calmly*) Oh, you mean *Reg*?

Patrick stares at her, frozen for a moment

Patrick You *did* see him!
Jenny Of course I saw him.
Patrick And ... and he saw you?
Jenny He couldn't miss me, could he? I was lying down on the sofa when he came in. (*She giggles*) I thought he was selling insurance!
Patrick (*doomed*) He found you ... lying down on my sofa with your legs?
Jenny Yes. It was ever so funny!
Patrick Yes, I'm sure it was ... !
Jenny He was so surprised to see me he practically had a fit!
Patrick Yes, I bet he did ... !
Jenny His face blew up like a balloon. I thought he was going to burst! (*She giggles, happily*)
Patrick You did explain to Reg that you were waiting for Trevor.
Jenny Well ... no.
Patrick (*wildly*) Then what the hell *did* you say to him?

Jenny settles herself more comfortably to explain

Jenny Well — he said he wanted to speak to *you*, so I told him that he couldn't at the moment because you were putting your clothes back on.

Patrick (*ashen*) What?!

Jenny Well, you were, weren't you?

Patrick Yes, but you didn't have to put it quite like that! Oh, my God — you've got to get out of here! I'll tell Trevor to come back and collect you. (*He goes to the telephone*)

Jenny No!

Patrick (*hesitating*) What?

Jenny I want to stay up here.

Patrick (*desperately*) But you don't belong up here! You belong down there! (*Pointing to the floor*) I'll call him. (*He starts to dial*)

Jenny But I don't want him to collect me.

Patrick You came here to see him!

Jenny Only because I knew where he lived.

Patrick Of course you knew where he lived! He chatted you up in Sainsbury's!

Jenny He lives in the flat under *you* ...

Patrick I know that.

Jenny (*pointedly*) So did *I* ...

Patrick stops dialling

Patrick What?

Jenny That's why I came here ... (*She smiles at him, enigmatically*)

Patrick holds her look for a moment, then puts down the telephone, nervously

Patrick I — I don't think I ——

Jenny I wasn't interested in *Trevor*. I wanted to meet *you* ... (*She gazes at him, adoringly*)

Patrick Well, of course you did! Everybody wants to meet me. But there's no need to go to such extremes. All you had to do was to apply to the ticket office in the usual way. Then you could have come to my show and seen me there.

Jenny But I wouldn't have seen you in your shorts, then, would I? *Or* had a lie-down in your bedroom.

Patrick Well ... no. No, you couldn't have done that, no. After all, the tickets are free. You can't expect to have *every*thing.

Jenny I haven't had *any*thing! Not yet, anyway ...

Patrick No, and you're not going to! Look — you really must go! (*He pulls her up from the sofa*)

Jenny But I promised Reg I'd join you both for drinks.

Patrick drops her back on to the sofa

Patrick Don't be ridiculous!
Jenny It's true. (*She looks about*) Where's he gone to, anyhow?
Patrick I'll tell you where he's gone to! He's gone to the pub on the corner
to think things over and make a decision, and then he's going to come back
here and fire me! (*He moves away, restlessly*)
Jenny Why should he fire you? I thought you were a star.

Which, of course, Patrick would never deny

Patrick Well ... yes. That's true. I am. Of course. But Reg is a very moral
man, so he's hardly likely to tolerate hanky-panky amongst his employees,
is he? And what happens? He comes here to discuss my future and finds
a sexy young girl with legs lying down on my sofa who tells him that I'm
out there putting my clothes back on!
Jenny You do think I'm sexy, then?
Patrick Of course I think you're ... That's got nothing to do with it! You can
imagine what he's thinking now!
Jenny Oh, no — everything worked out all right.
Patrick Did it?
Jenny I helped you out of a spot.
Patrick Did you?
Jenny And you should be grateful to me instead of being so cross.

Patrick stares at her blankly for a moment

Patrick What are you talking about?
Jenny Well, I knew what he was thinking, so I told him that I was ——

The doorbell rings

Patrick Oh, my God — he's here!

*He hastily pulls Jenny up from the sofa, and they both hop in unison to the
bedroom*

Jenny Where are we going?
Patrick *You're* going back into the bedroom!

He pushes her inside the bedroom and closes the door after her

The doorbell rings again

(*Muttering*) All right, all right, I'm coming ... (*He hastens to the door and opens it*)

Reg is there

(*Greeting him effusively*) Mr Godfrey? Do come in!

He ushers Reg into the room and closes the door

You didn't have to ring the bell, you know. The door wasn't locked.

Reg I'm not in the habit of walking into people's private property unannounced. Heaven knows what you might have been up to.

Patrick (*following him, nervously*) Oh, Mr Godfrey — you will have your little joke ... !

Reg It wasn't a joke.

Patrick Wasn't it? Oh, dear ...

Reg And you don't have to call me Mr Godfrey. If we're going to work together you must call me Reg.

Patrick Oh, thank you, sir.

Reg Just *think* of me as Mr Godfrey. (*Importantly*) I've been to the pub on the corner. (*He puts down his briefcase in the armchair*)

Patrick You didn't have to do that, Reg. I *can* afford a bottle of whisky! (*He laughs, playfully*)

Reg turns and gives him a stony look

Reg I needed time to think. After what *I* was told.

Patrick Oh, you mustn't believe everything you're told!

Reg (*grimly*) I might not have returned at all. After what *I* heard.

Patrick Well, I'm jolly glad you *did* return. Because I was here, sir — all ready and waiting! (*He smiles a sycophantic smile*)

Reg No, you weren't.

Patrick Sorry?

Reg You weren't here. You were out there. Putting your clothes back on!

Patrick Ah. Yes. But there was a good reason for that. I had to be prepared.

Reg (*appalled*) Prepared?

Patrick For you!

Reg I beg your pardon?

Patrick I was dressing for dinner. (*He pirouettes to show off his clothes*) For you.

Reg (*going to him*) I can tell you one thing, Sumner. You're a lucky man.

Patrick Am I? Oh, good. I wasn't sure.

Reg You've got one person to thank for my return.

Patrick Oh. Which person is that?

Reg Your wife!

Patrick Sorry?

Reg I only returned because of your wife.

Patrick My ... wife?

Reg Yes. We had a good long talk.

Patrick Er ... who did?

Reg Jenny and I, of course!

Patrick Ah — yes — well, I *can* explain about Jenny ——

Reg There's nothing to explain.

Patrick Isn't there? Oh, good. I thought there might be.

Reg It was Jenny who told me you were putting your clothes back on.

Patrick (*nervously*) I can't think why she told you that ... You might have wondered why I'd taken them off in the first place ...

Reg Presumably because you were going to have a shower. Or do you usually have a shower with your clothes on?

Patrick Ah — yes. Quite right.

Reg Well, I'm sorry about that.

Patrick About me having a shower?

Reg About me arriving early and catching you with your trousers down as it were!

Patrick Oh, they weren't down for very long!

Reg (*eyeing him suspiciously*) Long enough, I hope. I don't approve of people who skimp on cleanliness. (*He heads for the sofa*)

Patrick Oh, I never do that.

Reg It's next to godliness, you know.

Patrick Yes. It would be.

Reg Some people think they can make do with a lick and a promise by drenching themselves in toilet water. Eau Savage can cover a multitude of sins, you know.

Patrick I'm sure it can, sir.

Reg (*heavily*) But not on the sixth floor. (*He sits down*)

Patrick I should hope not!

Reg We're above that sort of thing on the sixth floor.

Patrick You're above most things on the sixth floor.

Reg The sixth floor can safely be said to be epitomized by two things — cleanliness and carpets.

Patrick And quite right, too!

Reg I beg your pardon?

Patrick I was agreeing with you, sir. Let me get you another drink.

Reg (*beadily*) I haven't *had* one yet.

Patrick Didn't you have one in the pub on the corner?

Reg I meant I haven't had one *here*!

Patrick No, of course you haven't. But you will?

Reg Of course I will!

Patrick Shall I pour it out for you?

Reg Unless you expect me to drink out of the bottle.

Patrick I meant—do you want it *now*? You don't want to freshen up—wash your hands — nothing like that?

Reg (*wearily*) Pour the drink, please, Patrick.

Patrick Pour the drink, please, Patrick.

Reg Whisky.

Patrick Whisky. Right. (*He goes to pour the drink*)

Reg Now, Sumner — there's something I want to talk to you about. Something that disturbs me very much.

Patrick turns, in a state of nervous apprehension

Patrick You're happy with my programme?

Reg No, no, no!

Patrick (*alarmed*) You're *not* happy with my programme? I'll change it! A little more music, perhaps? A juggler. Slack wire act. Something of that nature? (*He walks on an invisible wire*)

Reg I'm not talking about your programme!

Patrick Aren't you? Oh, good! I thought perhaps ——

Reg What's the matter with you? You seem very jumpy. Not sickening for something, are you?

Patrick I wouldn't be surprised ... !

Reg You know what I think? I think you've been spending too much time in the saddle.

Patrick Oh, I don't think so, Reg. It's a long time since I was on a horse. (*He laughs, nervously*)

Reg Not *that* kind of saddle! (*Indicating the exercise bicycle*) *That* kind of saddle!

Patrick Ah — yes.

Reg You know what that does to you, don't you?

Patrick (*ruefully*) Well, it is a bit uncomfortable ... (*He puts a comforting hand on his backside*)

Reg Saps your energy! Reduces your drive!

Patrick Does it, really? I'll sell it tomorrow. Your whisky, sir. (*He hands the glass to Reg*)
Reg Thank you. Aren't you joining me?
Patrick Yes. I've got one over here.

Patrick goes to his own drink — which is, of course, full to the brim. Reg eyes it, suspiciously

Reg Not hitting the bottle too hard, are you, Patrick?
Patrick (*looking at his very full glass*) It's ... it's mostly water, sir.
Reg It had better be! We don't encourage heavy drinking on the sixth floor. Cheers! (*He drinks, abruptly*)
Patrick Oh — yes ...

Patrick looks down at his glass. It is so full he is in danger of spilling it if he lifts it to his lips, so he ducks his head several times, gradually getting nearer to the glass. His nose is almost in the whisky when Reg speaks

Reg Sumner!

Patrick splutters into his drink and almost chokes. He withdraws his nose and tries to recover

Have you any idea what *I* was doing while you were putting your clothes back on?
Patrick Er ... how many guesses can I have?
Reg I was thinking things over.
Patrick Ah — in the pub — yes.
Reg Trying to come to conclusions. I've seen the career of many a good man ruined by a bad woman.
Patrick Is there one around here?
Reg One what?
Patrick A bad woman?
Reg It's no good pretending. I know all about it.

Patrick goes to him, anxiously

Patrick Ah — if you're thinking what I think you're thinking, there's a perfectly simple explanation.
Reg Walls have ears, Sumner. And eyes! *Media* ears and eyes. Tabloid ears and eyes! You and I know that. The merest breath of scandal about people in your position and suddenly we could be talking replacement!
Patrick Oh, we don't want to talk that, do we, Reg?

Reg However, I have decided to give you the benefit of the doubt.
Patrick Oh, good. I *am* glad.
Reg But only ——
Patrick (*quietly*) Yes, I *thought* there'd be a "But only ..."!
Reg But only because of your wife.
Patrick Oh. Good. I am grateful. And so will *she* be. When she hears about it. Benefit of the doubt about what?
Reg About the overflow!
Patrick (*blankly*) Overflow?
Reg From downstairs.
Patrick Sorry?
Reg The overflow from downstairs coming *up*stairs.
Patrick I didn't know overflows went uphill.
Reg This sort does, apparently. (*He leans forward, beadily*) The feminine sort!
Patrick Oh — *that* sort ...
Reg I shall overlook it this time.
Patrick Oh, good.
Reg On one condition.
Patrick Ah. What condition is that?
Reg That you take immediate action.
Patrick Oh, I will! Immediately! (*He sits down next to Reg on the sofa, eager for instruction*) What exactly did you have in mind, sir?

Reg glances around, elaborately, then leans forward to come almost nose-to-nose with Patrick

Reg Get a new lock for your door.

Patrick just stares at him for a moment

Patrick I beg your pardon?
Reg There are a lot of good firms about. Make excellent locks. Specialists. You know what I mean?
Patrick Oh, yes. Experts.
Reg Precisely. Consult. Take advice.
Patrick I will. Definitely.
Reg Keep out the riff-raff. Keep out the undesirables.
Patrick Oh, yes, rather! We don't want riff-raff. Not in here.
Reg You don't get riff-raff on the sixth floor.
Patrick Heaven forbid!
Reg It's nothing to do with heaven!

Patrick Isn't it?

Reg Organization. That's what it's to do with. That's how they manage to make the sixth floor what it is today. Free of riff-raff.

Patrick is a little puzzled as to the point of the conversation

Patrick Er ... was there some in here, then? Riff-raff?

Reg Certainly! So-called friend of yours. Lives downstairs. The flat downstairs. Or so he *says* ...

Patrick Oh — you mean Trevor?

Reg The window-cleaner?

Patrick No, no! Trevor's from the flat under this one.

Reg *Two* Trevors?

Patrick (*thoughtfully*) But I didn't know that he was riff-raff ...

Reg Walking about with a lady's handbag on his wrist! Then saying he was looking for a spare girl when he'd already got one! You can't afford to have riff-raff like that in your life, Patrick. It's bad for your image.

Patrick I suppose it is. I hadn't thought of that ...

Reg So first thing in the morning — on to the locksmith!

Patrick Absolutely. The minute I've finished my marmalade.

Reg gets up and moves away, pondering heavily

Reg Now, Patrick — about your programme ... (*He puts his glass down on the trolley, decisively*)

Patrick Ah — yes ... (*He leans forward, listening intently*)

Reg Is it to continue in its present form?

Patrick Well, *I'm* quite happy with it ——

Reg (*turning, thunderously*) That's what *I* have been brought in to decide!

Patrick Ah — yes, of course! And I'm sure you'll make the right decision, Reg.

Reg (*returning to him; profoundly*) There's only one Saturday in the week, Sumner. You and I know that.

Patrick (*quickly counting the days on his fingers and agreeing*) Yes — that's true!

Reg circles the sofa as he speaks, deep in contemplation

Reg So you're only seen on the television on one night in the entire week.

Patrick (*resentfully*) Yes. I hadn't thought of that ...

Reg I have decided that in future we shall do the programme *five nights* a week.

Patrick (*impressed*) Five nights a week? *What* a good idea!

Reg I had also decided to proceed with *you* at the helm as before ...

Patrick Oh, good! I *am* glad! That *is* a relief. I was beginning to think ——

Reg (*severely*) But that was before I read the newspapers.

Patrick (*looking at him in horror*) You haven't been doing that, have you?

Reg The question is — am I to take any notice of the notices? Are we people in positions of power to be influenced by media opinion? Am I to heed what the critics have been saying about you? Or can I be persuaded to ignore them?

Patrick I'm sure you *can*, sir! (*In his eagerness to please he slips off the sofa*)

Reg (*glaring at him on his knees*) I wouldn't be *too* sure, if I were you!

Patrick quickly resumes his seat. Reg continues circling the sofa

From now on we're moving the programme to an earlier hour. The family hour! That's why image is everything. You understand?

Patrick Nobody better.

Reg The question is, Sumner, are you the right person to captain the flagship of decency and decorum?

Patrick Well, I've always been a good sailor.

Reg We shall see, Sumner. We shall see ... (*Leaning forward suddenly, with an unexpected smile*) We don't need to be alone to talk business, do we?

Patrick (*staring at him, blankly*) Sorry?

Reg Why don't you fetch your wife out of the bedroom?

Patrick My ... my wife?

Reg Yes. She's in the bedroom.

Patrick No, no. She's in Paris.

Reg No. In the bedroom.

Patrick Yes. In the bedroom in Paris.

Reg No. In the bedroom here.

Patrick In the bedroom here?

Reg Yes.

Patrick She can't be!

Reg She is! (*He chuckles*) I should know. I put her there.

Patrick (*staring, blankly*) My wife?

Reg Yes.

Patrick gets up, nervously, and goes to Reg

Patrick You put my *wife* in the bedroom as well.

Reg As well as what!

Patrick As well as the other one.

Reg What other one? Pull yourself together, man. You've only got *one* wife,
    surely?
Patrick Yes, of course! So now they're both in there?
Reg No, no! Not both! Just one!
Patrick Just my *wife* in there?
Reg Of course.
Patrick But what about the other one?
Reg There isn't another one!
Patrick So there's only *one* in there?
Reg Yes, of course! Your wife!
Patrick My wife's supposed to be in Paris.
Reg But she didn't go to Paris.
Patrick Didn't she?
Reg Of course she didn't. (*He chuckles and drifts away*) She told me all about
    you, Patrick ...
Patrick Did she?
Reg I gather you're a bit of a romantic on the quiet. (*He sits in the armchair
    and gazes at Patrick in admiration*)
Patrick (*modestly*) Oh, I wouldn't say that exactly ...
Reg Jenny told me what you did when you spotted her kicking up her legs!
Patrick D-did she?
Reg (*with a big smile*) Every day for two weeks, eh?

Patrick considers this for a moment

Patrick Sorry?
Reg Must be a bit of a record. Mind you, it was only at the beginning, wasn't
    it? Don't expect it happens so often *now*? Just anniversaries and Mother's
    Day, I suppose? Ha! Ha! Ha! What beats me, Patrick — with all due respect
    — is how you got her to marry you in the first place.

Patrick goes to him, confused

Patrick I'm sorry. Who are you talking about *now*?
Reg Your wife, of course! She must be a good twenty-five years younger
    than you are.
Patrick Twenty-five years?
Reg If a day.
Patrick But I'm not even forty-eight yet!
Reg Oh, come on! Forty-eight?
Patrick Well ... forty-nine. But that's my last offer.
Reg Well, *she* doesn't look a day over twenty-three.

Patrick Twenty-three? My wife? What the hell has she been *doing* to herself in Paris?

Reg sets off for the bedroom

Where are you going?
Reg I'm going to fetch her, of course. You seem to have forgotten what your own wife looks like.

He goes into the bedroom

Patrick hastily takes a large sip from his over-full glass of whisky

Reg returns, carrying Jenny in his arms

Jenny smiles at Patrick, wife-like

Jenny Is it all right if I come in now, darling?

Patrick stares at her in horror

Patrick (*to Reg*) Is ... is *this* the one you were talking about?
Reg Of course it is! You haven't got another one, have you? Ha! Ha! Ha!

He puts Jenny down on the sofa

There you are, Mrs Sumner.
Patrick Look — I think there has been a slight misunderstanding here ...
Reg There's no misunderstanding, Sumner. Your wife and I have been getting along like a house on fire.
Jenny We hit it off right away. Didn't we, Reg?
Reg (*beaming at her*) We certainly did! With this little lady beside you, you'll go a long way, Patrick.
Patrick But *she's* not my —— ! (*He stops, uncertain of the best move*)
Reg Not your what?
Patrick Er — not my ... not my ... not my *second* wife.
Reg You said you hadn't *got* a second wife!
Patrick No — I haven't! (*Turning to her, desperately*) Tell him how you came to be in my flat!
Reg She's already done that. You spotted her in the chorus line.
Patrick What?!
Reg Kicking up her legs in tights! Ha! Ha! Ha!
Patrick (*to Jenny*) What on earth have you been telling him?

Jenny It's nothing to be ashamed of, darling. *I* think it was rather romantic. Surely you remember?

Patrick No, I don't remember!

Reg You sent her two dozen red roses.

Patrick Did I?

Reg Every day for two weeks!

Patrick So *that's* what you were talking about just now ...

Reg What did you *think* I was talking about?

Patrick Never mind—it doesn't matter ... ! (*To Reg, urgently*) Look—she's making all this up, you know. It isn't true!

Jenny He's so shy ... Isn't he adorable? (*She pats the side of Patrick's face, lovingly*) Patrick, darling, if I *was* making it up and I wasn't really your wife, Reg would wonder what I was doing lying down on your sofa when your wife was in Paris, wouldn't he? (*She smiles, pointedly*)

Reg Yes, he certainly would!

Patrick (*realizing*) Ah. Yes ...

Reg You know, Sumner, I have a feeling that this pretty little wife of yours is going to help me to ignore the stupid things the press have been saying about you ...

And Patrick, of course, always has an eye to the main chance

Patrick Really? (*He turns to Jenny with husbandly consideration*) Would you like a drink, darling?

Jenny Yes, please, Patrick. (*She smiles at him, triumphantly*)

Patrick Right. (*He sets off for the drinks trolley*)

Jenny I'd like my usual.

Patrick stops in mid-stride and looks back, uncertainly

Patrick What?

Jenny My usual ... darling.

Patrick Your ... usual?

Jenny Yes, Patrick. My usual.

Patrick You ... you don't usually have a usual.

Jenny (*acting hurt*) Oh ... you haven't forgotten my usual, have you?

Reg's bonhomie disappears as he moves behind the sofa to touch Jenny's shoulders, protectively

Reg I hope you haven't forgotten your wife's favourite aperitif, Patrick.

Patrick It does seem to have slipped my mind ... (*To Jenny*) Couldn't you give me a hint?

Reg It's the little things like that that separate the sheep from the goats.

Patrick Is it? I didn't know that.

Reg Oh, yes. The sheep are considerate. The goats are inconsiderate. Which are you, Sumner? A sheep or a goat?

Patrick I'm a sheep, sir! Definitely a sheep, sir!

Reg I hope so. A man in your position can't afford to be a goat.

Patrick I wouldn't dream of it. I've always been a sheep, sir. Always will be.

Reg Then I suggest you rack your brains and get your wife her favourite aperitif without further ado.

Patrick Yes, of course. I can't imagine how I could have forgotten. (*To Jenny*) I'll go and get your usual, darling. (*Quietly*) Oh, my God ... !

Patrick stomps away to the drinks trolley and proceeds to mix a drink into a cocktail shaker, pouring haphazardly from various bottles

Reg smiles warmly at Jenny

Reg He's a lucky man being married to you.

Jenny Oh, thank you, Reg ... (*She takes his hand*)

Reg It must be a constant source of comfort for him to know that you're always there in the background, supporting and encouraging him in his work.

Jenny Well, he's always very grateful. Aren't you, darling?

Patrick (*busy with the mixing*) Sorry?

Jenny You're very glad that I'm here, aren't you?

Patrick Oh, yes!

He puts the lid on the cocktail shaker and proceeds to mix it elaborately, whirling and bobbing like a Spanish dancer. Finally, he pours the liquid — which is red — into a glass and hands it to Jenny with a flourish

There you are, darling — your usual!

Jenny (*taking it*) Oh, thank you, darling! (*To Reg*) Doesn't that look lovely, Reg? (*She raises the glass*) Well — cheers!

Jenny takes a large sip and reacts to the horrible taste

Ooooh ... !

Patrick hovers, uncertainly

Patrick Is something wrong, darling?
Jenny What the hell did you put in it?!
Patrick I'm not quite sure. A little of this, and a little of that ...
Jenny It wasn't what I *wanted*! (*She puts the drink down on the sofa table, acting petulance*)
Reg Surely you haven't forgotten the ingredients of your own wife's favourite aperitif, Sumner?
Patrick No! No — of course I haven't! My hand must have been shaking.
Reg Shaking? Ha! Ha! You're not worried, are you?
Patrick Well ... yes, Reg. I am. Just a bit.
Reg Ah! About your future in television under our new dictum of decency?
Patrick Well ... yes. Frankly.

Reg looks from Patrick to Jenny, and smiles with confident approval

Reg Well, I think I can safely say ... that as long as Jenny's beside you ——

He hastily places Patrick firmly on the sofa next to Jenny and puts Patrick's arm around her, making a picture of a loving husband and wife

— and you're beside Jenny ... then you need have no worries about your future as a chat show host under *my* banner! (*He beams at them, approvingly*)

Trevor bursts in, talking as he arrives

Trevor Patrick, you're never going to believe what's happened downstairs!
Patrick And *you're* never going to believe what's happened *up*stairs ... !

Trevor sees Patrick and Jenny sitting cosily, side-by-side

Trevor Ah! You've come back again! What a bit of luck.

Patrick hastens urgently across to Trevor. Reg shuffles this way and that, impatiently

Patrick Will you please go away!
Trevor What are you talking about? I've come back for ——
Patrick Not now!!

Trevor stops, surprised by Patrick's vehemence

Trevor What?

Patrick You can't borrow any more sugar today!

Trevor I don't want to borrow sugar. (*He leans closer to Patrick*) It's all clear (*pointing to the floor*) down below.

Patrick I don't know what you're talking about.

Trevor Yes, you do!

He casts a quick smile across at Jenny, and then takes Patrick aside a little, confidentially

She's gone.

Patrick Who's gone?

Trevor (*whispering*) Virginia from Finsbury Park. I only popped out to the kitchen for a minute to warm up my wok, and when I came back she'd disappeared. So that's all right, then, isn't it?

Patrick No, it is *not* all right!

Trevor Don't be daft. Of course it is. (*He crosses to Jenny, playfully*) And where were *you* hiding yourself, eh? I've been looking for you everywhere.

Jenny stares at him as if he was a total stranger

Jenny I don't know what you mean.

Reg Neither do I!

Trevor jumps a mile

Trevor Oh, *you're* back, then? Did you have a good think in the pub? (*He laughs*)

Reg Yes, I did!

Trevor Well, I hope you came to the right decision. You shouldn't believe what you read in the papers. *I* think old Patrick's jolly good on the telly. Far from fading. Oh, and (*indicating Jenny*) you don't have to worry about *her*. It's not what it looks. I'm just going to move her. (*He prepares to lift Jenny*)

Reg *Move* her?!

Trevor Down to my place.

Reg What?!

Reg seeks solace by quickly getting a box of marshmallows out of his briefcase and desperately eating one

Patrick (*quietly*) Oh, my God ... !

Trevor (*to Jenny*) Patrick and I thought you might have got impatient and hopped off, but I'm jolly glad you haven't now that I've got things sorted out downstairs.

Jenny (*aloof*) I don't know what you're talking about.

Trevor Of course you do!

Jenny No — I don't.

Trevor Why are you playing hard to get all of a sudden? Surely you haven't forgotten what you came here for?

Patrick Trevor, will you please go back to your flat!

Trevor (*returning to Patrick, confused*) I thought you'd be glad to see me. We don't want him jumping to conclusions, do we?

Reg dithers across to Jenny with his box of marshmallows, takes one out and offers it to her

Patrick (*whispering, urgently*) It's too late for that ... !

Trevor Oh, dear. Does he think the worst?

Patrick Worse than the worst!

Trevor No problem. I'll get her out of your way. (*He goes back to Jenny*)

Patrick No! Trevor!

Trevor's arrival prevents Jenny accepting the marshmallow

Trevor Come on, darling — stop messing about — off we go!

Reg (*outraged*) How *dare* you speak to Jenny like that?

Trevor Jenny ... ?

Reg Barging in here acting like a savage! We're not used to savage behaviour on the sixth floor. (*He eats the marshmallow*)

Trevor All right, Reg — keep your knickers on.

Reg (*apoplectic*) Knickers?! (*He pulls up his jacket and stares at his trousers*)

Patrick intervenes, hastily

Patrick Trevor! I think you ought to go!

Reg You see what I mean about riff-raff?

Patrick I certainly do! (*He glares at Trevor*)

Trevor Who are *you* calling riff-raff?

Reg I'm calling *you* riff-raff!

Trevor I'm not riff-raff.

Reg Yes, you are!

Trevor (*to Patrick, rather hurt*) I'm not riff-raff, am I?

Patrick I'm afraid you *are*, Trevor.

Trevor I don't even know what riff-raff *is* ... You've never called me riff-raff before.

Patrick I've never *thought* of it before.

Reg I'm sorry for you, Jenny. It must be dreadful having neighbours like this. (*He puts the box of marshmallows back into his briefcase*)

Trevor (*to Patrick*) What's he on about?

Patrick I don't know ... !

Reg I don't like the look of him at all.

Trevor (*to Patrick*) Did you hear that?

Patrick Yes. He doesn't like the look of you at all.

Trevor Well, aren't you going to say anything?

Patrick I shouldn't think so.

Trevor Aren't you going to tell him what a nice chap I am?

Patrick No. Not at the moment.

Trevor Why not?

Reg Because you're not!

Trevor How do *you* know?

Reg If you were you wouldn't come bursting in here insulting respectable ladies on sofas!

Trevor (*laughing*) *She's* not a respectable lady!

Reg Patrick!

Patrick Y-yes, sir?

Reg Are you just going to stand there and let him talk about Jenny like that?

Patrick Well, I am thinking about it, sir ...

Trevor (*to Patrick*) What's it got to do with him how I talk about Jenny?

Reg You're not going to get away with it, you know. After tomorrow you won't be bursting in here again. Will he, Patrick?

Patrick He certainly won't, Reg.

Trevor Why? What's happening tomorrow?

Reg Action is being taken. Immediately.

Trevor (*to Patrick*) Action?

Patrick Yes, Trevor. We're taking immediate action.

Trevor Who is?

Patrick Well ... Reg and I ... and the locksmith.

Trevor Locksmith? What do you want with a locksmith?

Reg You'll soon see. The way will be barred!

Totally at sea, Trevor turns again to Patrick

Trevor What the hell's he talking about?

Patrick (*whispering, urgently*) Never mind! I'll tell you later!

But Trevor has had enough

Trevor Oh, no, you won't! I'm fed up with this. It's my turn now. (*He crosses to Reg*) Now, look here — *Reg* — you may put the fear of God into *him* but you don't bother *me* one bit!

Patrick Trevor! Please ... !

Trevor I came here to collect what I left behind and I'm jolly well going to collect it!

Patrick Oh, no ... !

Trevor She may *pretend* she doesn't remember but she remembers all right and as far as I'm concerned I'm going to carry on from where I left off!

Patrick But, Trevor, there's something you —— !

Trevor I've tidied up the flat, solved the over-crowding problem, warmed up my wok, and now I'm ready for *you*! So come on, darling! Let's go down to my place and get on with it!

He picks Jenny up in his arms. She struggles in vain, calling out. Reg looks appalled. Patrick wishes he was a million miles away

Jenny }   { Put me down! Put me down!
Reg }   (*together*) { How dare you! Now, look here —— !

Patrick and Reg look on in horror as Trevor heads for the door with Patrick's "wife" in his arms

They go, the door swinging shut behind them

Reg turns to look at Patrick in astonishment

Reg Aren't you going after him?!

Patrick Well, he did say it was his turn.

Reg (*appalled*) What?! That was your wife!

Patrick Oh — yes — so it was! Look — I can explain —— !

Reg This is no time for explanations! This is a time for action! (*He collects his briefcase*)

Patrick Reg, I promise you — there's nothing to worry about!

Reg (*apoplectic*) Nothing to worry about?! Nothing to worry about? You allow a sex-mad philanderer to march into your flat and carry off your own wife?

Patrick But Trevor's a good friend of mine ...

Reg That is no excuse! (*He starts to go*)

Patrick Where are you going?

Reg Back to the pub on the corner! I need more time to think. More time to make decisions. And when I return — *if* I return! — I hope you will have reclaimed your wife and put your house in order. We don't approve of wife-swapping on the sixth floor!

Reg goes abruptly, closing the door with a bang behind him

Patrick stands forlornly, for a moment, then finishes off his whisky and pushes the drinks trolley back to its original position. He crosses slowly with a heavy tread to his exercise bicycle. He pulls it into the room a little, climbs wearily into the saddle and starts to pedal in despair

The door opens and Kate comes in. She is an attractive, sophisticated woman of about forty-five. She is carrying a small travel bag and her handbag

Patrick does not see or hear her. He continues pedalling, intently. Kate closes the door, puts down her bag and crosses casually to him, watching his efforts with a smile

Kate Have you got as far as Knightsbridge yet?

Patrick slows down and stops pedalling. He turns slowly and sees her

Patrick Kate! You're supposed to be in Paris!
Kate (*with a big smile*) Oh, darling! I *knew* you'd be pleased to see me.

Patrick falls off his bicycle again

Black-out

ACT II

The same. A few minutes later

Kate is looking at Patrick with a big smile. He gets up from the floor, gazing at her in surprise

Patrick I thought you were in Paris!

Kate They cancelled the flight.

Patrick (*outraged*) They can't do that!

Kate They had no choice. French air traffic control are on strike. So if we *had* gone we'd have spent the whole evening flying around in ever-decreasing circles. And you know what that leads to. (*She puts down her things*)

Patrick So you decided not to go?

Kate Well, I'd have felt rather lonely without a pilot and crew. Did you know that the lock on this door isn't working? I got in without my key. *Anyone* could wander in.

Patrick Yes — they did ... !

Kate Who?

Patrick Er — Trevor!

Kate Oh, he's *always* popping in and out.

Patrick Yes. I'm sending for a locksmith in the morning. The minute I've finished my marmalade. Didn't they offer to put you up at the airport hotel? They usually do that.

Kate Patrick, aren't you pleased to see me?

Patrick Whatever gave you that idea?

Kate Because you fell off your bicycle.

Patrick That doesn't mean I'm not pleased to see you.

Kate Doesn't it?

Patrick No! I keep *on* doing it.

Kate Why?

Patrick I don't know.

Kate You're not usually a nervous sort of person.

Patrick (*flaring artistically*) Yes, I am! Just because I don't show it doesn't mean that I'm not! People don't realize how much we artistes give of ourselves. We may appear to be calm but inside we're *churning*!

Kate is somewhat taken aback by this outburst

Kate But why should you be churning tonight? You're not on the television now.

Patrick It — it was Trevor! He burst in and gave me a fright.

Kate I thought you'd be used to that by now. And nobody's forcing you to go bicycling in the sitting-room. You only do it because you're vain and you want to keep your figure.

Patrick You should be pleased! I'm trying to keep myself presentable for *you*! And for my public, of course.

Kate (*with a smile*) How nice of you to put it in that order, darling. I don't usually get better billing than your public. (*She sees Jenny's "usual" and picks it up in wonder*) Whatever's this?

For a moment Patrick is caught on the hop

Patrick It's Trevor's! He brought it with him. It's one of his health concoctions. You know he's always taking things to keep himself young and able.

Kate Perhaps *you'd* better try it, then, darling ... (*She hands it to him*)

Patrick (*with male pride*) There's nothing wrong with my performance! (*He puts Jenny's "usual" down on the drinks trolley*)

Kate There you are, you see — you're talking about your programme again! (*She settles herself on the sofa*)

Patrick sees that she is sitting down and races across to pick up the mobile phone, hopefully

Patrick Shall I telephone the airport? The strike may be over by now!

Kate Darling, they're not even having *talks* until tomorrow.

Patrick Aren't they? Oh. (*He puts the phone down, dismally*)

Kate So you may as well pour me a drink.

Patrick Are you going to *have* a drink?

Kate Yes, please.

Patrick Oh. Right. (*He sets off towards the drinks*)

Kate I'll have my usual.

Patrick stops and looks back at her, reacting to the word

Patrick Your ... usual?

Kate Gin and tonic, darling.

Patrick Ah. Yes. Of course. (*He goes to pour her drink*)

Kate You're all on your own, then?

Patrick Of course I'm all on my own! Why shouldn't I be all on my own?

Kate (*surprised by his vehemence*) I thought your new producer was coming over tonight.

Patrick Oh, him! Yes — yes, he ... he did pop in. Briefly. I — I'd forgotten all about it.

Kate He didn't stay very long, then?

Patrick No, he just ... popped in ... and popped out again. (*He gives her her gin and tonic*)

Kate Thank you, darling. Seems strange coming here to talk business and then leaving so quickly ... (*She sips her gin, thoughtfully*)

Patrick He was bleeped! Something unexpected had cropped up. And when you're bleeped you have to go. So he did.

Kate (*happily*) Oh, well ... never mind. Now we can have a quiet dinner together.

Patrick What?!

Kate Just the two of us ...

Patrick (*abruptly*) Didn't you get dinner at the airport?

Kate No. I thought I'd come home and have it with you.

Patrick Well, you can't! We've nothing in! The freezer's empty!

Kate Never mind. Let's have an early night instead. (*She leans forward and takes his hand*)

Patrick (*warily*) What?

Kate Well, if we aren't having food, we may as well go to bed and try to think of something else to do ... (*She smiles, encouragingly*)

Patrick (*his mind elsewhere*) Yes. You go ahead, darling. I'll be there in a minute.

Kate (*pulling her hand away, deeply insulted*) I'm not starting on my own!

Patrick But suppose Reg comes back?

Kate Why should he?

Patrick He ... he might have forgotten something.

Kate I can't think *what's* got into *you* tonight ... !

Patrick I — I've got one or two things to see to ...

Kate (*fed up*) Well, I don't care what *you're* going to do — *I'm* going to have a shower and go to bed. (*She picks up her travel bag and heads towards the bathroom with her gin*)

Patrick Wouldn't you prefer to go back and stay the night at the airport hotel?

Kate No!

Patrick I'll be happy to drive you there!

Kate (*disappointed*) Patrick ... !

Patrick French air traffic control may call off their strike first thing in the morning, then you'll be all ready for the first plane out!

Kate I did hope you'd be pleased to see me ...
Patrick I *am* pleased, darling! I was only thinking of you! It's a very
comfortable hotel at the airport. Much more comfortable than here!
Kate But I'd be on my own. I'll be *much* happier here with you.

*Kate smiles warmly and goes into the bathroom, closing the door behind
her*

Patrick No, you won't ... !

The main door bursts open and Jenny runs in

Patrick goes to her in a panic

You can't come in here!
Jenny Well, I'm not staying down there with *him*! (*She goes to the sofa*)

Patrick follows hastily, trying to quieten her

Patrick You must keep your voice down!
Jenny Why?
Patrick Well ... someone may be having an early night. (*He looks, anxiously,
towards the bathroom*)
Jenny (*looking about*) Where's Reg? He hasn't gone, has he?
Patrick Yes, he has!
Jenny I hope he's coming back.
Patrick *I* don't ... ! You shouldn't have told him that you were my wife!
Jenny Well, you didn't want him to think anything *else*, did you?
Patrick (*desperately*) But what's going to happen when my *real* wife turns
up?
Jenny You'll just have to keep her out of the way, won't you?
Patrick (*aside*) I may not be able to ... !

Trevor races in breathlessly and glares at Jenny

Trevor I thought you'd hurt your ankle!
Jenny (*remembering*) I have! (*She quickly stands on one leg*) Look — I'm
standing on one leg like a flamingo!
Trevor Well, you ran up those stairs like a gazelle!
Patrick Look — could you discuss wildlife somewhere else? (*He gives
another nervous glance towards the bathroom*)
Trevor (*to Jenny*) Why did you pretend?

Jenny Because I thought if I twisted my ankle and couldn't go home, you might find a nice, kind, honest, respectable, upright, good-natured, attractive, happily married, married man to look after me ...
Patrick (*helpfully*) I think she means me.
Trevor *You*?!
Patrick Ssh!
Jenny I think he's wonderful! (*She gazes at Patrick, adoringly*)

Trevor looks at Patrick in disbelief

Trevor *Him*?

Patrick shrugs

How did you know where he lived?
Jenny You told me.
Trevor Did I?
Jenny Last week in Sainsbury's.
Patrick (*going to him*) Oh, Trevor, I *am* touched! Fancy talking about me in the middle of Sainsbury's. (*Then, desperately*) Look, you really must go!

Trevor finds it hard to believe what he is hearing

Trevor (*to Jenny*) You mean ... you came to my flat ... because you wanted to meet *him*?
Jenny Yes. You see, when you thought you were chatting me up over the frozen fish, I was really chatting up *you* in order to meet *him*!

Trevor looks appalled

Can I help myself to a drink, Patrick? (*She goes to the drinks trolley*)
Patrick You haven't finished the last one yet!
Jenny No, and I'm not going to! (*She starts to pour a gin and tonic*)
Patrick (*whispering urgently, to Trevor*) You've got to get her out of here!
Trevor Why should I?
Patrick You said you were my friend.
Trevor That was before I knew she'd come to see *you*!
Patrick Look, Reg may be back at any minute! And Kate's in the bathroom!
Trevor *Your* bathroom?!
Patrick Yes!
Trevor *Your* Kate?!
Patrick Yes!

Trevor You said she was in France.
Patrick Well, she's not. She's in the bathroom!
Trevor Oh, my God ... !

Trevor runs across to Jenny, who is about to sip her gin

Come on, darling! Off we go again!

He picks Jenny up over his shoulder in a fireman's lift. She struggles. Patrick takes her drink as she is carried past

Jenny What are you doing? Put me down! Put me down!

Trevor carries Jenny out quickly

Patrick shuts the door after them, leans against it in breathless relief and drinks Jenny's gin and tonic

Kate comes out of the bathroom

She is now wearing a delightful dressing-gown and looks pretty good. Patrick hides the empty gin glass behind his back and tries to appear relaxed

Patrick Have a good shower?
Kate Yes, thank you.
Patrick You were very quick.
Kate Well, we don't want to waste any time, do we, darling? (*She goes to pick up her handbag from the sofa*) Did I hear voices just now?
Patrick V-v-voices?
Kate Yes. V-v-voices. In here.
Patrick I didn't hear anything!
Kate I was sure I heard people talking ... (*She goes towards the master bedroom*)
Patrick I expect your ears haven't adjusted to the change of altitude.
Kate (*turning back to face him*) Don't be silly, darling. I only got as far as the airport. My ears aren't usually affected by going up the escalator to the Duty Free.

She goes into the bedroom

Patrick puts down the empty glass. He gets a chair and puts it under the door handle to stop anyone getting in

Kate returns. Her attitude has changed — there is now a touch of ice in the air as she goes to Patrick

Darling ... ?
Patrick (*jumping with fright*) Aah! Yes?
Kate I ... I don't know how to put this, but did you know that there's a girl asleep in our bed?

Patrick stares at her blankly for a moment

Patrick What?
Kate A girl.
Patrick A girl? In our bed? You must have been mistaken.
Kate Patrick, I know what a bed looks like and I know what a girl looks like and there's one of each in our room.

A brief pause

Patrick (*hysterically*) My God! We've been burgled! (*He paces away below the sofa*)
Kate No, darling. When you've been burgled you *lose* something. We seem to have *gained* something.
Patrick But ... what's she doing in there?
Kate Well, the television was on so presumably she was watching it, got bored and fell asleep. Perhaps they were running one of *your* shows, darling! (*She smiles, sweetly*)
Patrick My shows do not send people to sleep!
Kate Yes, they do. One of the newspapers said they were more effective than Mogodon. Is this why you were so anxious for me to stay the night at the airport? I suppose three in that bed would be a *bit* cramped.
Patrick (*escaping*) I didn't even know she was in there!
Kate Then how did she *get* in there?
Patrick *I* don't know!
Kate Well, I'll leave you to sort it all out. (*She goes towards the spare bedroom*)
Patrick Where are you going?
Kate To make up the bed in the spare room!

She goes, closing the door noisily behind her

The doorbell rings

Patrick goes and whispers urgently at the closed door

Patrick Go away! You can't come in! Nobody can come in! I'm shut for the night!
Reg (*off*) I hope that doesn't apply to me, Sumner.
Patrick Oh, my God, it's God!

He hastily removes the chair and opens the door

Reg is there

(*Trying hard to appear pleased to see him*) Oh — oh, it's you, Reg! I — I didn't know if you'd be coming back.

Reg glares at him

But, of course, I'm jolly glad that you did!

Reg walks in past him, stony-faced, towards the exercise bicycle. Patrick closes the door and hovers, anxiously

Reg I hope you've got everything under control now.
Patrick I wish I had ... !
Reg What?
Patrick Of course I have!
Reg Everything shipshape and back to normal?
Patrick Oh, yes. (*He glances, nervously, towards the spare room and goes to Reg*) But — er — could we ... could we keep our voices down a bit? I've had complaints from the neighbours.
Reg The neighbours *this* way? (*He points* R)
Patrick No — the neighbours that way! (*He points* L) Two old ladies. Very light sleepers.
Reg Bit early for bed, isn't it?
Patrick Well, they like to go to bed early. So they can get up early. And walk. They like to get up early and walk.
Reg Hearing all right, then?
Patrick Yes, thank you.
Reg Not you! The old ladies!
Patrick Oh, yes. Clear as a bell. So if we could — er — keep it — you know — down a little — then they can get their beauty sleep and walk.
Reg I had no intention of shouting.

Patrick Oh, good.

Reg Got your wife back all right, then?

Patrick Oh, yes. Both of them ...

Reg What?

Patrick I mean — yes, I have!

Reg I can't understand you, Patrick.

Patrick I can't understand myself sometimes ...

Reg I'm a man who admires tolerance. Tolerance and understanding. Turn the other cheek. All that sort of thing. I'm a tolerant man myself.

Patrick I'm sure you are, sir.

Reg But I don't understand how you could let that — that riff-raff carry Jenny away. I'd never let a man carry *my* wife away.

Patrick (*surprised*) Wouldn't you?

Reg No, I wouldn't!

Patrick It ... it was just a bit of fun, that's all. Trevor only meant it as a joke.

Reg So where is she now?

Patrick Who?

Reg Your wife! Jenny!

Patrick Oh, *that wife* ... Ah — yes — well, she's she's lying down.

Reg Lying down?

Patrick Felt a bit faint.

Reg I'm not surprised after what she's been through.

Patrick So ... so that's that, isn't it?

Reg What's what?

Patrick Well ... we can't very well stay here — talking — not when my wife's feeling faint.

Reg No. I suppose not ...

Patrick So why don't we have dinner together? Out!

Reg And leave your wife lying down?

Patrick It was her suggestion.

Reg Was it?

Patrick Oh, yes.

He urges Reg towards the door

There's an excellent little French restaurant on the corner ...

Reg Well, I ... I *was* rather looking forward to talking to your wife ... And to *you*, of course!

Patrick I know you were, Reg. And she wanted to talk to you. And so did I! But she's really not up to it. Not tonight.

Reg What a pity.

Patrick Yes. So you go ahead.

He urges Reg further

It's called Le Bistro. Just on the corner. You can't miss it. Order yourself an aperitif. Anything you like. Campari. Champagne cocktail. Anything. I'll make sure my wife's got everything she wants and then I'll join you.

Reg I don't mind waiting.

Patrick Well, I'd rather you went ahead, Reg. They do get very busy at this time, so you grab a table and I'll join you as soon as I can. (*He opens the door*)

Reg Oh, very well. But don't be long. I'm not a patient man, Patrick. I'm liable to get itchy feet if people keep me waiting.

Patrick I'll be there on the double, sir.

Reg Right! (*He hesitates in the doorway*) I'm not at all happy about the lock on this door.

He goes

Patrick Neither am I ... ! (*He closes the door, gets the chair and puts it under the handle*)

He runs out into the main bedroom

After a moment, there is a female cry of surprise

Patrick returns, dragging Virginia after him. Virginia is a tall, languid blonde dressed in tight jeans and a revealing sweater. She wears glasses

Patrick Now! Who the hell are you and what are you doing in my bedroom?

Virginia I was just passing.

Patrick Just passing? I'm on the third floor! How did you get in there?

Virginia Up the fire escape and through the window.

Patrick (*apoplectic*) And into my bed?

Virginia Well, it was cold out there on the fire escape so I slipped under the duvet and it was so cosy that I must have nodded off. (*She peers at the exercise bicycle, short-sightedly*)

Patrick Right! (*He heads for the telephone*) You know what I'm going to do, don't you?

Virginia How many guesses can I have?

Patrick I'm going to telephone the police and tell them that you broke into my flat!

Virginia smiles, calmly, more interested in the bicycle

Virginia You think they'll believe you?
Patrick Why not?
Virginia Doesn't seem very likely.
Patrick You came in through my window! That's breaking and entering!
Virginia (*going to him*) Why should I want to break into *your* flat?
Patrick (*dialling*) Presumably because you'd seen me on the telly!
Virginia (*surprised*) Oh. Are you on the telly?

Patrick stops dialling, replaces the telephone and takes this body blow with as much fortitude as he can muster

Patrick You mean you've never seen me?
Virginia (*peering at him, short-sightedly*) I don't think so. Are you a policeman or a cowboy?
Patrick I am neither! I haven't got flat feet and I don't wear a big hat.

Virginia has a dreadful thought

Virginia Oh, my God, you don't read the news, do you? I never watch that.
Patrick (*smarting*) No, I do not read the news! You ... you really — truly — mean that you don't know who I am?
Virginia I've no idea.
Patrick But I'm on every Saturday night!
Virginia Oh, well — I'm out every Saturday night, aren't I? (*She notices that he has barricaded the door*) Why have you barricaded the door?
Patrick What? (*He looks*)
Virginia Was somebody trying to get in?
Patrick Yes — they *were* ... !

Virginia peers at the lock, short-sightedly

Virginia Wouldn't it have been easier to use the lock?
Patrick It's broken!
Virginia Oh, I see ... ! So when you found me asleep in your bed you put a chair there so nobody would interrupt us?
Patrick Well ... yes, but ——
Virginia Oh, good! Come on, then — *I* don't mind! (*She pulls him to the sofa and lies down, invitingly*)

Patrick hovers, nervously, appalled by her action

Patrick You can't lie down on my sofa!
Virginia Why did you barricade the door, then?

Kate comes out of the spare room and sees Virginia lying on the sofa

They look at each other in surprise

Patrick (*hissing at Virginia, urgently*) Sit up! Sit up!
Virginia What? (*She sits up and peers at Kate*)
Kate I don't suppose you find the sofa quite so comfortable as the bed?
Virginia Who are *you*?
Kate Did you solve the mystery, then, Patrick?
Patrick Yes! Yes, I did! She ... she came in through the bedroom window.
Kate Ah — like Peter Pan?
Virginia (*to Patrick*) What's she talking about?
Patrick *I* don't know!
Kate (*to Virginia*) I'm afraid he's rather cross with me. You see, I was
supposed to be flying to Paris tonight. Quite a coincidence, really, isn't it?
I was flying out, and you were flying in.
Virginia (*to Patrick*) I don't know what she's getting at.
Patrick *I* do ... !
Kate (*sweetly*) Have we discovered anything else about her, Patrick? Apart
from the fact that she flew in through the bedroom window.
Patrick I was just getting around to that.
Kate Yes. I thought you were getting around to *something*...

But Patrick is still smarting from the earlier wound to his pride

Patrick I simply can't believe that you've never seen me on the television ...
Virginia Well, I can't watch *every*thing, can I?
Kate Oh, dear. You mean to say that when he woke you up just now you
didn't ask him for his autograph?
Virginia I've never even *seen* him on the telly!
Kate No wonder he's looking so cross. (*She smiles, enjoying Patrick's
discomfort*)

Virginia has a sudden thought and turns to Patrick

Virginia Here — she's not your ... ?
Patrick Not my what?
Kate Oh, don't worry about me. I'm just passing through. (*She goes towards*

the main bedroom) I'm the Home Help. They always provide them for geriatrics.

She smiles sweetly at Patrick and goes into the bedroom

Patrick glares after her, then urgently makes his way to Virginia

Patrick What the hell were you doing out on the fire escape in the first place?
Virginia Trying to get back into Trevor's flat.
Patrick (*relieved*) Ah — you're Virginia! He *said* you'd disappeared.
Virginia Well, I ask you — chop suey and lager! That's not going to turn you on, is it?
Patrick Apparently not.
Virginia He was in the kitchen messing about with his wok so I popped out for some Kentucky Fried.
Patrick Down the fire escape?
Virginia Well, he'd locked the door and hidden the key. He always does that. It drives me mad. I mean, I'm not going to run away, am I?
Patrick But you did.
Virginia Only because I was hungry.
Patrick But why come up to *my* flat? I'm not a restaurant!
Virginia Well, you see, when I got back with the Kentucky Fried I couldn't get back in through Trevor's window. He must have locked that, as well! Then I remembered that he'd told me that he had a friend living up here. So I came up the fire escape, climbed in through the window and got into your bed.

Patrick gazes at her, stunned by this speedy exposition

Patrick You ate Kentucky Fried in my bed?!

Kate returns, carrying some bed linen, on her way to the spare room. She sees Virginia and reacts in mock surprise

Kate Oh — still here? Isn't it time you flew back to the Never-Never Land?

Patrick crosses to Kate, excitedly

Patrick It's all right! Everything's all right!
Kate (*coolly*) Oh, good. I'm so glad.
Patrick She's one of Trevor's! I should have guessed!
Kate I see. Just on loan. (*To Virginia*) They're very old friends. Lend each other anything.

Kate continues towards the spare room

Patrick (*desperately*) She's nothing to do with me!

Kate turns in the doorway and looks at Virginia with a smile

Kate I'm just making up a bed in the spare room. I do like to have plenty of space ready for unexpected guests, don't you?

She goes, closing the door behind her

Virginia She behaves more like a wife than a Home Help.
Patrick Yes, she does, doesn't she? I must speak to her about it.

The telephone rings. Patrick jumps, then answers

(*Abruptly*) Yes! What is it? What do you want? (*He softens his tone immediately*) Oh, it's *you*, Reg! ... Yes — yes — *I* thought I'd have been there by now, too. I'm so sorry. I got held up, you see. Did you get a table all right? ... Oh, good! And an aperitif? ... You've finished it. Oh. Well, get yourself another! Chew on a gris stick. I won't be long. (*Then, alarmed*) But I'll be there any moment. ... No — no, don't do that! I —— (*But Reg has hung up, so Patrick puts down the phone in despair*) Oh, my God! He's coming back!
Virginia Who?
Patrick Nobody *you* know. Come on!

He grabs her hand and leads her towards the bedroom

Virginia Where are we going?
Patrick Back to the bedroom.
Virginia Oo! Lovely!
Patrick And then *you're* going out of the window and down the fire escape.
Virginia What?!
Patrick You can't stay here!
Virginia Well, I'd rather go out *that* way! (*She sets off for the main door*)
Patrick No!

Patrick races around the sofa and intercepts her

Virginia Why not?

Patrick You might meet somebody coming in.
Virginia *I* don't mind!
Patrick Well, *I* do ... !

He leads her back into the room

Look, it's perfectly simple. You go out of the bedroom window, down the
fire escape and knock on Trevor's window.
Virginia He might not hear me.
Patrick Well, knock loudly! (*He urges her on her way*)
Virginia No — I'd rather go this way!

*She escapes from him, runs away below the sofa and round to the door again.
He races after her. She giggles, dodging this way and that, trying to elude
him. But he catches her*

Patrick Come on — quickly!

He pulls her across towards the bedroom door

Virginia But I don't like heights!
Patrick You didn't mind coming up.
Virginia It's different going down!
Patrick Well, you should have thought of that before.

*He pulls her out, protesting, into the main bedroom, closing the door
behind them*

Kate comes out of the spare room

Kate I've made up the bed in there so ... (*She stops, seeing nobody there*)

*The doorbell rings. Kate goes to the door. She reacts to the barricade, moves
it, and opens the door*

Reg comes in and sees her

And she sees him. Neither knows who the other is

Reg Who are you?
Kate I'm his wife.
Reg Not *another* one!

Kate (*puzzled*) I'm sure he only put *one* wife down on the Electoral Register ...

Reg closes the door and glares at her

Reg You needn't pretend! Patrick's wife is in the bedroom! (*He marches down to the sofa*)
Kate (*following him, amused*) Oh, is *that* who he told you she was?
Reg Did he know you were coming?
Kate No. I arrived unexpectedly half an hour ago.
Reg Didn't take you long to get your clothes off, did it?
Kate Well, there was no food in the freezer, you see, so we thought we'd have an early night. You know how it is ...
Reg No, I do *not* know how it is! Patrick was supposed to be having dinner with *me*!
Kate He never mentioned it.
Reg (*glaring at her*) No — he had other things on his mind! (*He puts his briefcase in the armchair*)
Kate I'll give him a shout. Who shall I say it is?
Reg Reg Godfrey!
Kate Oh, I thought *you*'d been and gone.
Reg (*surprised*) You mean you've heard of me?
Kate Oh, yes. Patrick told me all about you.
Reg Talks to you about his programme, then?
Kate (*wearily*) Oh, yes — all the time ... And you really mustn't take any notice of what those silly newspapers have been saying about him.
Reg Never mind what they've been saying about *him* — if the tabloids get to know about *you* they'll have a field day!
Kate (*smiling, modestly*) Oh, they wouldn't be interested in *me* ...
Reg They would if they found out what's going on here! (*He sits down in despair*)
Kate Oh, Reg, I wouldn't tell them about that! What do you think I am?
Reg You mustn't ask me that ... !
Kate Patrick said you'd popped in earlier, but I didn't know he'd arranged to meet you for dinner.
Reg I've been waiting in the bistro on the corner!
Kate I wish I'd known. We could *both* have joined you. I was quite hungry until I got my mind off food and on to sex.
Reg (*appalled*) How you can talk like that when *she's* lying down in *there*?!
Kate (*going to him, furiously*) You mean she's lying down again?
Reg Had to, poor kid. Felt a bit faint.
Kate I'm not surprised, climbing up the fire escape like that.

Reg (*puzzled*) Sorry?
Kate Anyway, how did *you* know about her being in the bedroom?
Reg Patrick told me, of course! That's why I went on ahead to the bistro.
Kate Well, I'll tell him you're here. (*She starts to go towards the bedroom*)

Reg leaps up and pursues her

Reg You can't go in there!
Kate Why not?
Reg He won't want Jenny to see you! (*He pulls her back into the room*)
Kate Jenny? Is that her name?
Reg Yes.
Kate *You* seem to know more about her than *I* do.
Reg Well, he's hardly likely to tell *you* about her, is he?
Kate (*grimly*) No — you bet he isn't! (*She starts to go again, blazing*)
Reg (*catching her again*) No! You mustn't!
Kate It's all right. Patrick should have got rid of her by now.
Reg (*appalled*) Got rid of her?!
Kate Well, she's not staying here, I can tell you that ... !
Reg Now, look here, young lady —— !
Kate Oh, thank you, Reg. That *is* kind ...
Reg I don't want you spoiling things for them.
Kate Why not? They've been spoiling things for me!
Reg That's hardly the same thing, is it? They make a fine couple, and I don't want someone like you coming in and rocking the boat.
Kate It's not the *boat* I'm going to rock ... !
Reg With Jenny beside him he's going to go a long way.
Kate Yes, and the sooner the better ... !
Reg She's such a very pretty young lady ...
Kate (*seething*) Yes, I know! Tall and blonde!
Reg Tall and blonde? Small and dark!
Kate Small and dark?
Reg Yes.
Kate Good heavens! There must be another one about!

Patrick comes in, breathless. He sees them

Patrick Oh, my God ... ! (*He starts to go out again*)
Kate Patrick!

Patrick puts on the brakes

Don't go away ...

Patrick (*nervously*) W-what?
Kate It's all right. You can come in.
Patrick Oh. Right. (*He shuffles, anxiously*)
Kate Did you get rid of Peter Pan?
Patrick It was a bit of a struggle but I managed.
Kate Oh, good. Because now Captain Hook's arrived! (*She looks at Reg*)

Patrick hastens around the sofa to greet Reg and shake his hand, enthusiastically

Patrick Ah! Hallo, Reg! I didn't want you to come back here ...
Reg No. And I can see why! (*He glares at Kate*)
Kate Patrick, you're quite *sure* the one in there has gone?
Patrick Yes. I took her down the fire escape.
Reg (*appalled*) Down the fire escape?!
Kate Oh, good! Because Reg has been telling me all about the *other* one!

She sets off towards the spare room

Patrick Where are you going?
Kate *I* shall sleep in the spare room!

She goes, shutting the door with a bang

Reg moves away, restlessly

Reg I'm disappointed in you, Sumner ...
Patrick My ratings haven't gone down, have they?
Reg It's nothing to do with your ratings! It's your private life that seems to be in disarray.
Patrick But, Reg — surely it's programme ratings that matter?
Reg We didn't care about ratings in Religious Broadcasting. It was the message that mattered. And my message to you is that a man's public image is in direct proportion to his private life. And if a man's private life falls below the standards we require, then I would not hesitate — nay, I would rejoice! — in cutting that man to the ground! (*He strikes one hand with the other, decisively*)
Patrick Yes, I think you would ... !
Reg How could you send your poor little wife away like that?
Patrick Sorry?

Reg advances as his anger mounts, causing Patrick to retreat

Reg You told me that she was lying down in there feeling faint, and in spite of that you've sent her packing to make room for another woman! And you wouldn't even let her use the lift!

Patrick collapses into the armchair, falling on top of Reg's briefcase

(Fearing for his marshmallows) Aah! (*He grabs his briefcase and moves away, examining the contents anxiously*)

Patrick follows him, nervously

Patrick Well, I ... I didn't actually send her packing, Reg. She ... she had a little lie-down, and ... and suddenly felt better — much better. So — as you and I had decided to eat out — she ... she popped out to ... to visit her mother.
Reg Leaving you alone with the other one? (*He protects his briefcase from Patrick and takes it back to its resting place in the armchair*)
Patrick Er ... which other one is that?
Reg The one in the spare room!
Patrick Ah — er — yes ...
Reg (*pondering, powerfully*) I came here tonight to discuss the future of your programme. And — more importantly, perhaps, Sumner — *your* future. (*He settles on the sofa*)
Patrick Yes, I know you did, Reg ...
Reg And it doesn't appear to me as if your private life will stand up to careful scrutiny.
Patrick Won't it? Oh, dear. I did hope it would.
Reg We don't approve of shady backgrounds in television.
Patrick Is that what I've got?
Reg It's beginning to look like it! Packing your sick wife off down the fire escape to her mother so that you can bring a loose woman into your flat.
Patrick Er ... which loose woman are we talking about?
Reg The one in the spare room!
Patrick Oh, you mean Kate?
Reg Is that her name? She had the nerve to pretend to be your wife — to *me*!
Patrick Oh, dear. Is that what she told you?
Reg But I knew better, didn't I? I know a liar when I see one ...

Patrick flinches under Reg's penetrating gaze

Patrick Yes, I — I'm sure you do!

Patrick decides to regroup his forces in the interests of survival, and sits beside Reg

Patrick (*diplomatically*) Reg ... I think there has been a — how can I put this? — a slight ... misunderstanding here.
Reg Misunderstanding? I doubt it.
Patrick H-h-h-how ... how did she put it exactly?
Reg Who?
Patrick Kate. About being my wife.
Reg She said, "I'm his wife", of course!
Patrick "I'm his wife"?
Reg Yes.
Patrick She didn't say, "I'm Patrick's wife"?

Reg considers

Reg N ... no.
Patrick Ah. Well, there you are!
Reg What?
Patrick (*expansively*) Kate is nothing to do with me.
Reg Nothing to do with you?
Patrick No.
Reg She seems to be sleeping in your flat!
Patrick Ah — yes — but that doesn't mean anything.
Reg Doesn't *mean* anything?!
Patrick Good heavens, no! (*He prepares to deliver the coup de grâce*) You see, when Kate said, "I'm his wife", she didn't mean *my* wife, she meant ... *his* wife.

Reg considers again

Reg Whose wife.
Patrick Trevor's wife.
Reg *Trevor's* wife? (*Astounded*) Kate is the wife of the riff-raff downstairs?
Patrick Yes.
Reg Then what is she doing up here?
Patrick (*heavily*) I ... I didn't want her to find out about him. About the life he leads.
Reg I can understand that ... !
Patrick I was just on my way out, you see — to join you in the bistro — when Kate arrived home and couldn't get into their flat ... (*leaning forward dramatically*) because he'd locked the door! And you know why ...
Reg I can guess!
Patrick He had another woman in there.

Reg That's what I guessed. The man's insatiable!

Patrick So ... I invited Kate up here. What else could I do, Reg? I pretended that Trevor was out and told her that she could stay here.

Reg All night?

Patrick (*with a generous shrug*) If necessary. That's why she's making up a bed in the spare room.

Reg Yes, she *said* she was going to have an early night ...

Patrick Well, she'd had a tiring day. She needed rest. I didn't know then, of course, that Jenny would be going off to see her mother.

Patrick sighs, impressed by his own performance. Reg lets the new truth sink in, and takes Patrick's hand

Reg (*remorsefully*) Patrick ... what must you think of me?

Patrick (*generously*) It was understandable, Reg. Quite understandable. (*He pats Reg's hand*) I forgive you.

Reg (*moved*) Thank you, Patrick. But I feel ... unworthy of forgiveness. When I think of the things I said to that poor woman ...

Patrick (*momentarily confused*) Er ... which poor woman is that?

Reg The one out there! Kate! *His!*

Patrick Oh, don't worry about her. She'll get over it.

Reg I can never forgive myself ...

Patrick (*patting his hand again*) *You* don't have to, Reg. *I've* already done that.

Kate enters from the spare room, carrying her toothbrush, and sees them holding hands

They hastily let go of each other

Kate Excuse me. I'm just going to brush my teeth.

She heads for the bathroom. Reg leaps up and quickly goes to her

Reg Kate!

Kate stops, surprised by his familiarity

Kate I beg your pardon?

Reg What can I say?

Kate I think you've said enough already.

Reg Yes. I have! That's the trouble.

Kate Then in that case I suggest you don't say anything else and allow me to continue on my way to the bathroom.

Patrick (*rising, anxiously*) Yes, Reg! Let her go to the bathroom.

Reg But you see, I didn't know!

Kate Didn't know what?

Reg That you were his wife.

Kate I told you I was.

Reg Yes, but I thought you ——

Patrick I think you ought to let her go to the bathroom, Reg!

Reg How could you marry a man like that?

Kate I'm beginning to wonder. (*She glances at Patrick, meaningfully*)

Kate tries to continue to the bathroom but Reg runs around the exercise bicycle and intercepts her

Do you mind? I'm trying to get to the bathroom.

Reg He's not worthy of you!

Kate No. I know. But he's all I've got.

Reg Well, I should get rid of him, if I were you.

Kate It had crossed my mind ... (*She darts another look at Patrick*)

Reg There are better men about, Kate. You wouldn't have to look far. You're a very attractive woman.

Kate Well, thank you, Reg. That's very kind of you. But now I really must go to the bathroom.

Patrick Yes. You'd better let her go. It might be important.

Reluctantly, Reg stands aside to allow her to pass. Kate looks at Patrick, severely

Kate *You*'re not off the hook, though!

She goes into the bathroom, shutting the door with a bang

Reg looks at Patrick, puzzled

Reg What did she mean by that?

Patrick I've no idea ... !

The door to the corridor bursts open and Trevor comes in, carrying a protesting Jenny

Jenny Put me down! Will you put me down!

Reg cannot believe his eyes. Patrick is in despair

Reg I thought she'd gone to see her mother?
Patrick Yes! She had!
Reg Well, *he* doesn't look like her mother, does he?
Patrick (*desperately*) Trevor — where did you find her?
Trevor What are you talking about? (*He goes to put Jenny down on the sofa*) I didn't find her anywhere!
Patrick (*to Reg, nervously*) I expect he was lying in wait for her outside and pounced on her as she left the building!
Trevor (*going to Patrick*) Have you gone mad?
Reg You poor kid ... (*He hastens across to sit beside Jenny and offer comfort*)
Jenny Oh, Reg ... ! (*She falls into his welcoming arms*)

Patrick drags Trevor aside a little and whispers to him, urgently

Patrick You said you'd keep her out of the way! You can't bring her back in here! Not *now*!
Trevor I had no choice. Virginia's trying to get back in through the window!
Patrick Well, don't let her in!
Trevor I *want* to let her in now I know Jenny's only interested in *you*!
Patrick Is this what you call friendship? Couldn't you have been celibate just for one night?
Trevor And break the habit of a lifetime?
Reg My God, I admire you, Patrick.
Patrick Oh, thank you, Reg.
Reg If I was in your position I wouldn't be able to control myself.

Patrick, as always, has an eye to the main chance

Patrick Ah, but Reg — a man who couldn't hide his emotions — a man unable to keep control — would hardly be the man for five nights a week, would he?

Reg looks at him with even greater admiration

Reg Right! Point taken. Like it! Like it!
Trevor Well, *I* don't hide my emotions and *I'm* all right for five nights a week. In fact with a few words of encouragement I can manage twice on Saturday and a midweek matinée!

Reg is appalled by such coarseness

Reg You see what I mean by riff-raff. (*He gets up, moves away towards the armchair and snaps his fingers, imperiously*) Patrick!
Patrick (*turning, surprised*) I beg your pardon?
Reg Over here! (*He beckons*)
Patrick Oh. Right. (*To Trevor*) I'll be back in a minute.

Patrick trots, dutifully, across to Reg, who takes him aside a little

Reg (*conspiratorially*) Don't forget who's in the bathroom ...
Patrick I wish I could ... !
Reg We don't want Kate finding out about her husband, do we?
Patrick (*alarmed*) No, we certainly don't!
Reg So you'd better get him out of here — double quick!
Patrick What a good idea. (*He trots back to Trevor*) There! I wasn't very long, was I?
Trevor No. I hardly missed you.
Patrick You'd better get out of here — double quick!
Trevor That's what I was trying to do! (*He starts to go*)
Reg And think yourself lucky to have got away with it so lightly.
Trevor (*hesitating*) Got away with what?
Reg Trying to seduce Patrick's wife!

Trevor stares at him, blankly, for a moment. Patrick wishes he was a million miles away

Trevor I beg your pardon?

Patrick grabs Trevor and pushes him towards the main door again

Patrick I thought you were going? It's time you were going!

Trevor frees himself from Patrick's clutches and looks across at Reg

Trevor Seduce Patrick's wife?
Reg Yes!
Trevor (*bemused*) But I've never even touched his wife! Well, I may have given her a quick kiss on the cheek at Christmas. Under the mistletoe. But it's never been a meaningful relationship. No offence, Patrick. She's a very attractive woman. But she's yours, and I wouldn't.
Reg But you tried to! Downstairs!

Trevor Don't be daft! I was downstairs with Jenny.

Reg Exactly! And you were trying to reduce her!

Trevor What if I was? Jenny's not Patrick's wife.

Reg Of course she's Patrick's wife!

Trevor (*blankly*) I beg your pardon? (*He turns to Patrick*) You're very quiet.

Patrick I'm composing a symphony. (*He conducts, briefly*)

Trevor (*going to Jenny*) Did you hear what he said?

Jenny Yes. He's composing a symphony.

Trevor Not him — *him*! (*He points at Reg*)

Jenny Oh. Yes, I heard him.

Trevor So haven't you any comment to make?

Jenny What about?

Trevor Well, if somebody came in here and said that I was the Prince of Wales I think I'd deny it!

Jenny But you're *not* the Prince of Wales.

Trevor Exactly! That's the point I was trying to make.

Reg But she *is*!

Trevor Don't be silly. I know she's not the Prince of Wales! She's not even the Princess.

Reg But she *is* his *wife*!

Trevor Come off it! I know his wife and she's not a bit like Jenny.

Exasperated, Reg hastens to his briefcase and seeks solace once more in his marshmallows

Trevor Patrick!

Patrick (*cowering, nervously*) Hm?

Trevor For heaven's sake tell this idiot that Jenny's not your wife!

Patrick Of course she's my wife!

Trevor stares blankly at Patrick for a moment. Reg starts eating a marshmallow

Trevor Patrick ... I know you'll think I'm being very stupid and all that, but there does seem to be some confusion here ...

Patrick (*wildly*) There's no confusion! She's my wife and that's all there is to it.

Reg You see? What did I tell you? (*He puts the marshmallows back into his briefcase*)

Trevor (*to Patrick, suspiciously*) What the hell are you up to ... ?

Reg moves away a little and snaps his fingers imperiously again

Reg Patrick!

Patrick (*turning, surprised*) I beg your pardon?

Reg Over here!

Patrick Oh. Right. (*To Trevor*) Here I go again ... (*He trots across to Reg as before*)

Reg (*conspiratorially*) I'm very worried about the bathroom ...

Patrick Yes, so am I ... !

Reg So get your friend out of here ...

Patrick He's no friend of mine ... !

Reg I'll try and keep her in the bathroom until he's gone. (*He puts his briefcase down in the armchair*)

Patrick No, no — you stay here, Reg! I'll go to the bathroom.

Trevor (*going to Jenny, thoughtfully*) Jenny ... I seem to have forgotten — how long have you and Patrick been married?

Jenny } (*together*) { Six months.
Patrick }   { Three years.

Trevor What?

Jenny } (*together*) { Three years!
Patrick }   { Six months!

Trevor (*sorrowfully*) And I never sent you a present ...

Reg (*aside to Patrick*) Get him back to his flat! I'll keep Kate in there as long as I can. (*He goes towards the bathroom*)

Patrick But Reg —— !

Reg (*to the others*) I'm just going to the bathroom.

Trevor Oh, good. Have one for me.

Reg goes into the bathroom

Trevor crosses to Patrick, who cowers nervously

Now! What the hell was that all about?

Patrick Reg wanted to go to the bathroom. (*He escapes around the sofa*)

Trevor (*pursuing him*) About you and Jenny being married!

Patrick Well, it was all *your* fault!

Trevor *My* fault?!

Patrick It was you who left Jenny on my sofa in the first place.

Trevor But I didn't tie a label round her neck saying, "This is Patrick's wife", did I? So whatever gave him that idea?

Jenny I *told* him.

Trevor You didn't!

Patrick She *did*! *And* she told him that I first met her when she was a dancer in the chorus!

Trevor You didn't!
Jenny I did!

Trevor laughs, noisily. Patrick glares at him

Patrick It's not funny!
Trevor Oh, yes, it is! I think it's very funny! Anyway, why didn't you deny
  it?
Patrick (*blankly*) What?
Trevor Why didn't you tell Reg that it wasn't true?

Patrick edges away, uneasily

Patrick Well, I ... I couldn't disillusion him, could I?
Trevor I bet it was to your advantage.
Jenny Yes. Reg thinks I make you a lovely wife — and that you'll go far so
  long as *I'm* beside you... (*Draped on the sofa, she smiles at Patrick,
  adoringly*)
Patrick Anyway, it's too late to tell him *now*!
Trevor (*going to Patrick*) But what are you going to do when he *does* find
  out?
Patrick He mustn't find out! If he discovers that Jenny isn't my wife he
  won't hesitate — nay, he will rejoice! — in cutting me to the ground! (*He
  hits one hand with the other to demonstrate, and hurts himself*) Ooh!

  Kate comes in from the bathroom

Kate Will you please tell Reg that I do not need a chaperon when I'm
  cleaning my teeth.

*She storms off towards the spare room but stops when she comes face-to-face
with Jenny*

Jenny Who are you?
Kate I'm Kate! Who the hell are *you*?

  *Reg comes in from the bathroom. His glasses are slightly out of position
  and he is holding one hand to his face*

Reg (*to Patrick*) It's no good. I couldn't keep her in there. (*He adjusts his
  glasses*)
Kate You certainly tried hard enough. Is that how they behave in Religious
  Broadcasting up in Scotland?

Reg I was trying to comfort you.

Kate Oh, is that what it was? You've got more hands than an octopus. (*Surprised to see Trevor*) Hallo, Trevor!

Trevor Hallo!

Reg (*hissing at Patrick*) You didn't get rid of him!

Patrick He wouldn't go ...

Reg Well, it's too late now! (*He goes to Kate, heavy with sympathy*) I ... I expect you're surprised to see him here.

Kate Trevor? No. He often pops up to see Patrick.

Reg I mean ... *tonight.*

Kate (*with a smile*) Oh — well, yes, I suppose he *is* usually busy downstairs at the weekends! (*She grins at Trevor*)

Reg (*glaring at Trevor*) And *you* must be surprised to see *Kate* here!

Trevor (*with a shrug*) No, not really.

Patrick Yes, you are, Trevor!

Trevor No, I'm not. You told me she was here.

Reg Dressed like that? And coming out of Patrick's bathroom?

Trevor I expect she's going to have an early night.

Kate I was but people keep arriving ...

Jenny (*bewildered*) Who is this lady?

Kate (*sitting beside Jenny*) And who is *this* lady?

Reg Surely you two know each other?

Jenny No.

Reg (*thinking he knows the reason*) Ah, yes — of course — I suppose you're such a busy woman you're hardly ever at home to meet the neighbours. This is Kate.

Jenny Yes, but why is she coming out of the bathroom dressed like that?

Reg looks at Patrick and sighs, heavily

Reg I'm afraid we can't escape the truth any longer, Patrick ...

Patrick Can't we? What a pity ...

Reg (*to Jenny*) You see, Patrick didn't want her to know.

Kate Didn't want me to know what? About *her*, I suppose! (*She glares at Jenny*) I'm not surprised!

Reg No, not about her — about *him*!

Kate Who?

Reg Trevor!

Trevor (*surprised*) Me?

Reg (*heavily*) He didn't want you to know about Trevor ...

Kate Good heavens, I've known about Trevor for years!

Reg About ... about what goes on ... downstairs?

Kate Yes. Everybody knows about that. He's famous for it. Aren't you, Trevor?

Trevor (*modestly*) Well, I ... I put it about a *bit*, I suppose ...

Reg (*to Kate*) And you don't mind?

Kate No. He can do what he likes. It doesn't bother me.

Patrick has become frozen with fear as impending doom approaches

Reg You hear that, Patrick?

Patrick stares at him blankly for a moment

Patrick Er ... sorry?

Reg She knows about Trevor and she doesn't mind.

Patrick D-doesn't she?

Reg (*to Kate*) You see, we didn't know that you knew about Trevor. That was why Patrick invited you to come up here and sleep in the spare room.

Kate I'm sorry, I don't quite ...

Trevor Yes, *I've* lost track of the conversation, too ... !

Reg You see, he was there all the time.

Kate Patrick?

Reg No — Trevor! In the flat downstairs.

Trevor Of course I was. That's where I live.

Patrick I told you he wasn't there! Don't you remember?

Kate No ...

Patrick Yes, you do!

Kate No, Patrick, I don't. I don't even know what you're talking about.

Reg (*as to a child*) Trevor ... wasn't ... out.

Trevor Of course I wasn't. I was warming up my wok.

Reg He was down there all the time. When you tried to get into the flat he wasn't out at all. He was there! With another woman ...

Trevor What the hell's that got to do with you?

Kate gets up and goes to Patrick, bemused

Kate And why on earth should I try to get into Trevor's flat? I'd far rather be up here with you.

She links her arm through his

Reg begins to inflate

Patrick No, you wouldn't! (*He extricates himself*)
Kate What?
Patrick You wouldn't!
Kate Yes, Patrick, I would! In spite of whatever you've been up to today, I'd rather be here with you than down there with Trevor any day.
Patrick No, you wouldn't! You'd rather be down there with him! You know you would!
Kate It's not like you to be so modest. And with all due respect to Trevor I do prefer to be with you.
Reg (*to Kate, regretfully*) If this is how you treat your husband I don't *blame* Trevor for going off with other women ...

Kate and Trevor both look puzzled

Trevor Er ... Patrick ... ?
Patrick What *now*?!
Trevor What's he talking about?
Kate Yes — that's what *I* want to know!
Jenny So do I ... !
Patrick (*miserably*) I wish you'd all go away and leave me to ride on my bicycle ...
Kate Reg, I think you're a little confused.
Trevor }
Jenny } (*together*) So am I ... !
Kate I'd rather be with Patrick than with Trevor, and that's all there is to it. And that is why I am sleeping up here with *him* and not down there with *him*!

Reg, horrified at what Jenny is hearing about her "husband", tries again to restrain Kate's apparent indiscretions

Reg You mustn't speak like that! Not in front of Jenny! (*He sits beside Jenny, comfortingly*)
Kate Ah! So *she's* Jenny? I should have known. Small and dark.

She turns to look at Patrick with a smile that could slice bacon

So this is the other one? No wonder you didn't introduce us ...
Patrick W-what?
Kate Reg told me how well you go together and what a perfect couple you make! (*She marches off towards the spare room*)
Patrick But you don't understand —— !

Kate storms out into the spare room and slams the door behind her

Jenny *(bewildered)* Who *is* that lady?

Reg hastens to reassure her

Reg Oh, you don't have to worry about her.
Jenny Don't I?
Reg Oh, no. Things look much worse than they really are.
Patrick *(quietly)* I wish I could believe that ... !
Reg She's only sleeping here.
Jenny Sorry?
Reg In the spare room.
Jenny But why is she sleeping here at all ... ?
Reg *(imperiously)* Trevor!
Trevor *(leaping to attention)* Sir!

Reg goes to Trevor

Reg *(importantly)* This is the time to redeem yourself.
Trevor Is it? I didn't know that.
Reg So don't hang about here. Go after Kate!
Patrick I don't think she *wants* Trevor to go after her.
Reg Oh, yes, she does! She may think she doesn't, but she does. *(To Trevor)* Off you go! *(He urges him on his way)*
Patrick But she may be catching a plane first thing in the morning!
Reg There's always another plane, Patrick. Life is more important than flight departures.
Trevor But she'd rather be with Patrick — she *said* so!
Reg Now, look here — there are some things that only a husband can say to his wife.

Trevor is puzzled. Patrick starts to climb on to his exercise bicycle

Sumner! This is no time for pedalling!
Patrick Oh, yes, it is! I know when it's pedalling time and this is it! *(He pedals, wearily)*
Reg *(imperiously)* Trevor!

Trevor leaps to attention once again

Trevor Sir!

Reg Surely you're not going to leave Kate up here in *this* flat when she should be down there in *your* flat?

Trevor But why should Kate be down there in my flat?

Reg Good God, man! She is your *wife*!

Trevor freezes. Jenny rises in surprise

Trevor My *wife*?!

Jenny You never said you had a wife!

Trevor goes around the exercise bicycle to look into Patrick's face

Trevor Patrick ... !

Patrick (*innocently*) Hm?

Trevor Tell them ...

Patrick Hm?

Trevor Tell them I haven't got a wife.

Patrick falls off his bicycle. He gets up from the floor in a highly nervous state and rattles away at the astonished Trevor

Patrick Of course you've got a wife! How could you forget you've got a wife? I don't forget I've got a wife, so why should you forget you've got a wife? (*To Reg*) You don't forget you've got a wife, do you, Reg?

Reg Certainly not!

Patrick (*to Trevor*) There you are, you see! Reg has got a wife. I've got a wife. You've got a wife. We've all got a wife. Not just one wife. One wife each. We've each got a wife. Three assorted wives. One for me, one for Reg and one for you. You may think you haven't got a wife. You may sometimes wish you hadn't got a wife. But you've got a wife all right and don't you forget it!

Trevor gazes at Patrick in bewildered silence for a moment

Trevor It's a funny thing, you know. I can't recall the ceremony. Was it a church wedding? Or a registry office?

Reg (*to Trevor*) I hope you're not the sort of man who runs away from responsibility? We never run away from responsibility on the sixth floor.

Patrick I should hope not. It's a long way down.

Reg sets off towards the spare room, grimly

Where are you going?

Reg I think it's time Kate knew exactly what sort of a man she's married to.

He goes into the spare room

Trevor goes to Patrick, menacingly. Patrick cowers, apprehensively

Patrick I — I can explain ...
Trevor (*looking at his watch*) Well, you've got exactly thirty seconds on your specialized subject and the time starts now!
Patrick Ah. Yes. Well, there was a strike. You see? Air traffic. No control. So no planes. Result. Kate here. Not there. Reg meets Jenny. Jenny speaks. "Me wife". Reg sees Kate. Dressed for bed. Conclusion obvious. Kate fringe benefit. Reg disapproval. Sixth floor — never! All that. Explanation needed. Explanation found. Frantic.

Trevor looks astonished

Trevor You call that an explanation?
Patrick I had no choice! I had to tell Reg that Kate was married to you. I couldn't let him think I was having a bit on the side. It was the only thing I could think of.
Jenny You mean ... Kate's *not* married to Trevor?
Patrick Of course not!
Jenny Then who *is* she married to?
Trevor To Patrick, of course!

Jenny is horrified. She runs to Patrick

Jenny I thought your wife was in Paris.
Patrick So did I!
Jenny Oh, my God ... !
Patrick But you mustn't let Reg know. As far as he's concerned Kate's married to Trevor!
Trevor You really expect me to go through with this charade?
Patrick Trevor, that's what friends are for.
Trevor So what do you want me to do? Carry Kate out of here and take her down to my flat? (*With a smile*) Actually, that might not be a bad idea ...
Patrick What?
Trevor Well, I've always rather fancied Kate. And if you're going to hand her over to me on a plate I'm not going to say no, am I?
Patrick You don't have to go to extremes! Just take her down to your flat, give her a cup of tea and explain the situation to her.

Trevor (*grinning*) If I take her down to my flat I'll give her more than a cup of tea!

Patrick You don't imagine for one minute that Kate would even look at you?

Trevor Don't you be too sure. Women who are married to older men quite often fancy a bit of younger stuff. (*He leans against the bicycle, preening himself*)

Patrick I am not older men!

Kate comes in from the spare room, followed by Reg. She is looking far from pleased

Jenny looks apprehensive

Kate Will you please tell Reg that he may now reign supreme on the sixth floor but it does not give him the right to come barging into my bedroom!

Reg I did knock.

Kate But *I* didn't say "Come in"! Patrick, I have taken two sleeping pills and I must be left alone. (*She starts to go*)

Reg But he's come to take you home!

Kate I beg your pardon?

Reg Your husband has come to take your home.

Kate I *am* at home!

Jenny (*unhappily*) I wish *I* was ... (*She sinks on to the sofa*)

Patrick She's confused, poor thing.

Kate I am nothing of the sort.

Patrick You shouldn't have taken sleeping pills. They've made you disorientated.

Kate goes to Patrick in a daze

Kate Patrick, the evening has already been bad enough. I came home to find a strange girl on the sofa and another in our bedroom. I have carried sheets and pillow cases from one room to another like a maid in a French farce and now I am told that I can't go to sleep in the spare room because somebody wants to take me home!

Jenny I wish somebody would take *me* home ...

Kate You stay there! I'm coming to you in a minute! (*To Patrick*) What the hell is going on?

Reg Is this the way you repay Patrick for his kindness?

Kate What kindness? The only person Patrick's ever kind to is himself.

Patrick On the contrary, I'm kind to lots of people.

Kate Who?

Patrick Er ...

Kate Well?

Patrick Give me a chance! I'll think of somebody ...

Reg After all, he took you in when Trevor was keeping you out. Isn't that something to be grateful for?

Patrick The vicar's wife!

Kate What?

Patrick I was kind to her only the other day. She came out of Sainsbury's and dropped three packets of fish fingers and a toilet roll. And *I* helped her pick them up!

Kate Only because you are angling for the OBE.

Patrick You don't get the OBE for picking up toilet paper!

Kate I'm very surprised. They seem to give them for everything else. (*To Reg*) Why should I give a damn whether Trevor's keeping me out of his flat or not? He's over-subscribed already.

Jenny (*helpfully*) But I'm sure he loves you really!

Kate Oh, Trevor ... And you never said. Did you hear that, Patrick? Trevor loves me. Isn't it touching? (*She turns to glare at Jenny*) How the hell do *you* know?

Jenny Er ... Patrick told me.

Kate Oh, *did* he? (*She turns to glare at Patrick*)

Patrick Of course he loves you!

Kate Sorry?

Patrick Well, it would be very unnatural if he didn't! (*Going to him, pointedly*) Trevor — I thought you were anxious to go ... ?

Trevor (*blankly*) What?

Patrick pushes him towards Kate

Ah — yes — right! (*He quickly goes to Kate; romantically*) Now then, Katie darling — you come downstairs with me ...

Kate (*after a stunned silence*) Trevor, my birthday's not until *next* week. Why don't you save the surprises till then?

Patrick (*to Trevor*) Go on, then! Don't hang about!

Trevor All right! All right! I'm doing my best. (*To Kate*) Come along, darling. The flat's not far away.

Kate I know where it is but ...

Trevor Well, come on, then!

Kate (*starting to feel sleepy*) But I'm in my night-dress.

Trevor That's all right. We don't want to waste any time, do we?

Kate I think I must have taken too many sleeping pills. I don't know what anybody's talking about ...

Reg Trevor — you're a lucky man.
Trevor Am I? Oh, good. I wasn't sure.
Kate Patrick, will you please send all these people away. I want to go to bed.

Reg intervenes with authority and crosses to Kate

Reg Now, look here, Kate — I don't want to be severe, but if you're going to bed at all you're going to bed with Trevor!
Kate Am I?
Reg Of course you are!
Kate (*to Trevor*) Am I?
Trevor Of course you are!
Kate Oh. Well, I suppose it'll make a change ...
Reg Trevor's reformed, you see. Haven't you, Trevor? He's given up all his other women and from now on he's only going to sleep with *you*.
Kate Well, that's very nice of you, Trevor. I'm very flattered. It's a sweet thought and I do appreciate it. But I hope you won't be offended if I say that — in all truthfulness — I'd rather sleep with Patrick.
Patrick No, you wouldn't!
Kate Yes, I would. Honestly.
Patrick No! You may think you would but you wouldn't! A lot of people think they'd like to sleep with me. They see me on the television and they think they'd like to sleep with me. But they wouldn't! Not really!
Reg Kate ——!
Kate You keep out of this! Who I go to bed with is *my* affair!
Reg But think about Jenny! Think how *she* feels! How would you like to be in her position?

Jenny cries, noisily. Kate looks at her, briefly

Kate I don't know what position she's in. I only know that I'm tired and I want to go to bed ...
Trevor Come with me, then! (*He tries to lead her away*)
Kate (*extricating herself*) No! I prefer to be with Patrick. (*So she goes to him*)
Patrick No, you don't! Trevor's much better than I am. He's younger than I am, he's better looking than I am ——
Kate Good heavens, Patrick. You must be ill to talk like that. (*She closes to him, fondly*) Oh, darling, I didn't mean the things I said about your programme. I love it. I really do. And your performance is incredible.
Reg (*to Jenny*) Don't listen to her! Just cling on to me and close your ears!

Jenny cries again as Reg sits beside her, protectively

Kate (*to Reg*) What's so terrible about me wanting to be with Patrick? I thought you of all people would approve of that.

Reg Not when you're already married to another man!

Kate looks puzzled

Kate What other man?

Reg Trevor, of course!

Kate turns slowly to look at Patrick. He cringes and smiles, nervously

Patrick I ... I did try to keep it a secret.

Kate And as far as *I'm* concerned you succeeded! (*She goes to Reg*) Reg ... if I'm married to Trevor, what am I doing sleeping in Patrick's flat?

Patrick intervenes, desperately

Patrick The Isle of Wight!

Kate What?

Patrick That's where you did it. On the ferry. In front of the captain.

Kate Where we did what?

Patrick Got married.

Kate Who?

Patrick You and Trevor!

Kate Me and *Trevor*?

Patrick Yes.

Kate (*turning to him*) Trevor ... ?

Trevor I *think* it was the Isle of Wight ...

Kate But I've never *been* to the Isle of Wight!

Patrick Oh, yes, you have! You spent your honeymoon in Sandown on a yacht. Bobbing up and down in the Solent.

Kate (*thoughtfully*) I'm sure I'd have remembered ...

Reg (*rising, angrily*) Kate, do be reasonable! You and Trevor go back to your flat downstairs and leave me to talk over the future with Patrick and Jenny.

Kate turns to look at Patrick. He smiles, nervously. She turns back to Reg, bemused

Kate Patrick and *Jenny*?

Jenny That's *me* ... (*She starts to cry again*)

Kate I don't know why *you* keep crying! I'm the one who should be upset. (*To Reg*) What the hell has Patrick's future to do with *her*?

Reg Well, it's not unnatural for a wife to be interested in the future of her own husband!

A dreadful silence

Patrick starts to tiptoe away

Kate Where are *you* going?
Patrick A walk? It's a lovely evening ...
Kate Stay where you are!

Patrick stays where he is, fearfully

(*Turning to Reg again*) What are you talking about?
Reg Don't you understand? (*Indicating Jenny*) This is Patrick's wife!

Patrick and Trevor are in despair. Kate looks at Jenny with a lethal smile. Jenny's tears are frozen

Kate Well ... ! And *I* never knew! Patrick, darling, why didn't you tell me?
Patrick I-I-I-I-I Oh, my God ... !
Reg That's what I was trying to tell you in the bathroom.
Kate Oh, is that what you were doing? I did wonder.
Reg We've got plans for Patrick up on the sixth floor.
Kate (*glaring at Patrick*) So have I — and the higher the better! (*She crosses to Trevor, a determined glint in her eye*) Come on, then, Trevor! Let's go downstairs and get on with it!

She links her arm through his. Trevor grins at Patrick, and shrugs, world-wearily. They start for the door. Patrick suffers in silence. Jenny jumps up, desperately

Jenny No!!

Kate and Trevor stop and turn. Patrick and Reg gaze at Jenny in surprise

Kate Oh, good — you've stopped crying. That *is* a relief.
Jenny You can't go with him!
Kate Why not?
Jenny Patrick doesn't want you to!
Kate Oh, I thought he did ...
Reg Of course he does!

Jenny (*to Reg, sharply*) You keep out of this!
Reg I beg your pardon?! (*He sinks on to the sofa*)
Jenny (*going to him*) Stop her, Patrick!
Patrick Sorry?
Jenny Stop her going with Trevor.
Patrick Ah. Yes. Well ...
Kate You see? You can hardly expect him to stop me going off with my own husband. (*To Trevor*) Come along, darling! I'm getting cold ...
Trevor We'll soon change all that ...

He grins, lecherously, and they start to go again

Jenny (*louder*) No!!!

Kate and Trevor hesitate

Kate Whatever's the matter? I thought you'd *want* to be left alone with Patrick. After all, he is your husband.
Jenny It's no good. I can't go through with it. (*To Reg*) He's *not* my husband!
Reg (*rising*) What?
Patrick Oh, my God ... !
Kate I must have misunderstood. Reg, you *did* say that Jenny was Patrick's wife, didn't you?
Reg Yes, I did!
Jenny Well, I'm not! (*She looks at Patrick, adoringly*) I only wish I *was* ...

Reg looks at Patrick, ominously

Reg Well, Sumner?

Patrick starts to shake

What have you got to say for yourself?

Patrick nods, defeated

Patrick Jenny's right. She's not my wife.
Reg Then whose wife *is* she?
Jenny (*unhappily*) I'm nobody's wife ... (*She cries*)
Trevor (*unhappily*) Neither am I ... ! (*He cries with Jenny*)
Reg Don't be silly. Kate's your wife!
Kate No, I'm not. I'm Patrick's wife!

Reg (*to Patrick*) You said she was (*indicating to Trevor*) *his* wife!
Patrick I know I did.
Reg (*to Jenny*) And *you* said you were Patrick's wife!
Jenny I know I did ...
Reg (*to Patrick*) And *you* didn't deny it!
Patrick I know I didn't ...
Reg Deception!
Patrick I suppose so ...
Reg Intrigue!
Patrick If you say so ...
Reg We don't like deception and intrigue on the sixth floor, Sumner. A man who goes in for deception and intrigue is not the man I'd trust with five nights a week in the family hour! (*He decisively marches away to get his briefcase from the armchair*)
Patrick (*quietly*) That's what I was afraid of ... !

And at this moment Virginia walks in from the bedroom

Virginia Is it all right if I get back into your bed for a bit?

They all look at her in surprise, except for Reg, who perches on the edge of the armchair and busies himself with his briefcase

Kate (*going to her*) Well! If it isn't Peter Pan! Back from the Never-Never Land! If you're looking for the Lost Boys they're over there. (*Indicating Patrick and Trevor*)
Jenny Who does *she* belong to?
Patrick Well, she doesn't belong to me!
Kate What a pity. I thought you were collecting them.
Virginia (*crossing to Trevor*) Why didn't you let me back in? Didn't you hear me tapping on the window?
Trevor (*innocently*) Oh, it was you? I thought it was a seagull.
Patrick No. Another sort of bird.
Jenny Are you a friend of Trevor's, then?
Virginia (*glaring at him*) Not any more!

Virginia turns away from Trevor and sees Reg for the first time. Puzzled, she goes to look at him more closely. Reg opens his briefcase in the hope of not being seen and takes out a marshmallow

Don't I know you?
Reg (*eating his marshmallow*) No — I don't think so — no ...

She turns his face round and recognizes him

Virginia Well! What a lovely surprise ... !
Reg Marshmallow? (*He offers her a marshmallow*)
Virginia Reggie — *darling*!

They all look at Reg in surprise

Patrick Don't tell me you two know each other?
Virginia We certainly do!

She pulls Reg to his feet and tried to cuddle him but he keeps his briefcase between them

How nice to see you again! Why didn't you get in touch with me?
Trevor It sounds as if that's what he *has* been doing!
Jenny You're very quiet, Reg.
Patrick He's trying to remember the Lord's Prayer.
Kate (*moving down to Reg and Virginia*) Where did you meet him, then?
Virginia At a telly conference in Scotland. I was doing the catering and we got talking. You know how it is.
Patrick We're beginning to find out!
Virginia And the next day he picked me up in his car and showed me the Highlands. (*She giggles*) Amongst other things ... !
Reg Oh, my God ... !
Patrick You can tell he used to be in Religious Broadcasting. (*Going to Reg, his confidence flooding back*) Reg ... you weren't up to hanky-panky in the Highlands, were you?
Virginia He certainly was!
Patrick I thought you didn't approve of hanky-panky.
Jenny What would your wife say if she knew what you'd been up to?
Patrick Just what *I* was thinking!

Reg seethes

Virginia Oh, Reggie, isn't this lovely? We can have a nice reunion.
Trevor Good idea! You can take her out to dinner.
Patrick Go to the bistro on the corner! I expect they've still got our table.
Virginia How about it, Reggie darling?

Reg knows he is a defeated man

Reg Oh, very well ...
Virginia Super!

She starts to lead him towards the main bedroom but Patrick stops her

Patrick (*smiling, generously*) Oh, no, Virginia! Not down the fire escape. *This* time you can use the lift.
Virginia Oo — thanks!
Trevor This way, Reggie darling!

He opens the door with a big smile, relieved to be getting rid of Virginia. Virginia leads Reg to the door

Patrick By the way, Reg ...
Reg (*warily*) Now what?

Patrick tries hard to hide his smile of triumph

Patrick It looks as if we'll have to postpone our business chat, doesn't it? We wouldn't want to spoil your reunion with Virginia, would we? Shall I ... shall I pop up and see you on Monday morning?
Reg (*glaring at him*) I'll see you in ... ! (*He stops*)
Patrick Yes?
Reg (*changing his tone*) I'll see you on the sixth floor. (*He turns to go, a beaten man*)
All Good-night, Reggie!

Reg and Virginia go

Trevor closes the door after them. Patrick moves to the sofa in relief

Patrick Well! I'd never have thought that of Reg ...
Kate *I* would! I knew what he was like the minute he tried to get hold of my toothbrush.
Jenny I wish he'd taken *me* out to dinner. I'm starving.
Trevor (*going to her*) Well, now Virginia's out of the way, why don't I take you downstairs and show you my wok?
Jenny Your what?
Trevor My wok! I'm a dab hand with Chinese food.
Jenny Well, I am rather hungry.
Trevor Say no more!

Jenny goes to Kate

Jenny Goodbye, Mrs Sumner.
Kate (*with a smile*) Kate. Goodbye, Jenny.

Jenny turns to Patrick and looks at him, a little sadly

Jenny Goodbye, Patrick. It was ever so nice being married to you.

Patrick smiles, affectionately

Patrick It was ever so nice being married to you, too. (*He kisses her gently*)

Jenny starts to go but is so overcome by the kiss that she loses her balance and twists her ankle

Jenny Ooo!

Patrick and Trevor support her

Now I really *have* sprained my ankle!
Trevor That's all right. I'm used to carrying you now. (*He picks her up and sets off for the door*)
Jenny But if I've sprained my ankle how am I going to get home?
Trevor Who said anything about going home?
Trevor } (*together; to Patrick and Kate*) Good-night!
Jenny }
Patrick } (*together*) Good-night!
Kate }

Trevor carries Jenny out

Patrick closes the door and turns to look at Kate with a hopeful smile

Kate (*abruptly*) Good-night!

Kate marches out into the spare room and slams the door

With a heavy tread Patrick goes to his exercise bicycle and climbs on to it, despondently. He starts to pedal, rather too energetically

Kate reappears

Kate Have you got as far as Knightsbridge yet?
Patrick (*pedalling, furiously*) No! I'm still in the middle of the park!

Kate smiles and goes to put the chair up against the door to prevent anyone getting in. Then she crosses to the master bedroom and turns in the doorway

Kate Patrick ...

Patrick stops pedalling and turns, breathing heavily, to see what she wants

Patrick Hm?
Kate Why don't you leave the last few miles until tomorrow? You don't want to tire yourself out, do you?

She smiles provocatively and disappears into the bedroom

Patrick falls off his bicycle. He gets to his feet, unsteadily. He tries to follow her but though the spirit is willing, too much energetic pedalling has paid its price and he staggers, weak at the knees. Then he notices Jenny's "usual" on the trolley. He picks it up, looks at it for a moment, then drinks it down in one go. He reacts to its biting potency, then begins to smile as he finds that it perks him up no end

There are a few bars of "hurry" music as he makes his way with increasing speed and optimism into the bedroom and slams the door behind him

Black-out

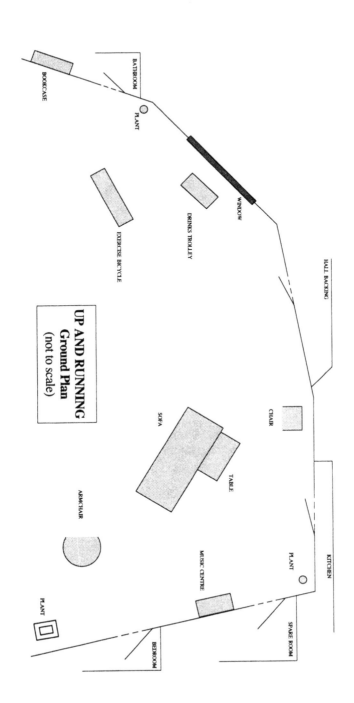

UP AND RUNNING
Ground Plan
(not to scale)

BOOKCASE

BATHROOM

PLANT

WINDOW

EXERCISE BICYCLE

DRINKS TROLLEY

HALL BACKING

KITCHEN

SPARE ROOM

PLANT

BEDROOM

MUSIC CENTRE

PLANT

ARMCHAIR

SOFA

TABLE

CHAIR

FURNITURE AND PROPERTY LIST

ACT I

On stage: Sofa. *On it:* coloured cushions
Armchair
Sofa table. *On it:* mobile telephone, writing pad, biro
Upright chair
Drinks trolley. *On it:* whisky, gin, orange juice, tomato juice, tonic
    water, cloth, various glasses, cocktail shaker, dish of nuts, jug of
    water
Exercise bicycle. *On it:* towel
Bookcase. *In it:* books
Potted plants

Off stage: Handbag (**Jenny**)
Tray of ice cubes (**Patrick**)
Ice bucket (**Patrick**)
Briefcase containing papers, box of marshmallows (**Reg**)
Handbag (**Kate**)
Travel bag (**Kate**)

Personal: **Reg**: spectacles

ACT II

Off stage: Bed linen (**Kate**)
Toothbrush (**Kate**)

Personal: **Virginia**: coloured-rimmed spectacles

LIGHTING PLOT

ACT I

To open: Full stage lighting; summer evening effect

Cue 1   **Patrick** falls off his bicycle again   (Page 41)
           Black-out

ACT II

To open: As for ACT I

Cue 2   **Patrick** hurries into the bedroom   (Page 85)
           Black-out

EFFECTS PLOT

ACT I

Lightning Source UK Ltd.
Milton Keynes UK
UKHW021443190522
403241UK00009B/41

9 780573 019166